Scripture and the Skeptic

Scripture and the Skeptic:
Miracles, Myths, and
Doubts of Biblical Proportions

978-1-7910-0421-7
978-1-7910-0422-4 *ePub*

Also by Eric Huffman

40 Days of Doubt:
Devotions for the Skeptic

978-1-5018-6913-6
978-1-5018-6914-3 *ePub*

Miracles, Myths, and Doubts
of Biblical Proportions

SCRIPTURE
AND THE
SKEPTIC

ERIC HUFFMAN

Abingdon Press

Nashville

SCRIPTURE AND THE SKEPTIC

Library of Congress Control Number: 2020949129
ISBN-13: 978-1-7910-0421-7

Contents

Prologue 9

1. Isn't the Bible Only Human? 17

2. Is the Bible Fact or Fiction? 39

3. Are the Gospels Reliable? 61

4. What Is the Bible About? 81

5. Why Is the Bible So Messy? 103

6. Is the Bible Racist? 129

7. Can We Talk about Leviticus? 151

8. Why Is the Bible So Backward? 179

Conclusion 197

Resources for Personal Reflection and Group Discussion 203

Notes 217

PROLOGUE

Defining moment

Finding the drawer full of teeth was the point of no return along my journey into cynicism. I was eight or nine years old when, while ransacking my mom's bedside table in search of loose change because the ice cream truck was fast approaching, I happened upon a plastic bag with almost a dozen familiar baby teeth. *My* teeth. The teeth my mom swore the *Tooth Fairy* so desperately wanted. What was I supposed to believe now—that the Tooth Fairy swiped those teeth from under my pillow and then left them in Mom's drawer? *That's ridiculous,* I reasoned. *Why would the Tooth Fairy pay me good money for teeth and then turn around and give them to Mommy?*

Something wasn't adding up. After running through all the possible scenarios in my head—*Mommy bought my teeth back from the Tooth Fairy, Mommy stole my teeth from the Tooth Fairy, Mommy is the Tooth Fairy*—logic led me to one painfully obvious conclusion.

Mommy lied about the Tooth Fairy.

Looking back, I think a switch flipped in my heart that day; from then on, I was paranoid about all things supernatural. I became the preeminent anti-Santa crusader in my fourth-grade class. My school occasionally invited magicians to entertain the student body, but while other kids seemed to enjoy the swindler's tricks, I hyper-analyzed every sleight-of-hand until I could debunk them all.

Amplified by adolescence, my cynical edge grew louder and meaner in the 1990s. Most people were shocked when they heard that the guys from Milli Vanilli were lip-syncing the whole time,[1] but not me. *I knew something wasn't right about those guys.* And when the obviously guilty Hall of Fame running back got off scot-free after killing his ex-wife and her boyfriend? *I called it.* When others were scandalized by the proliferation of steroids in our national pastime, I wore my Sammy Sosa jersey with pride. *Who cares? Everybody was doing it.* And when the president lied about what he did in the Oval Office with the intern in that blue dress? *So what? Politicians lie all the time.*

Just like my mom, about the Tooth Fairy.

The only reason I'm telling you this is so you'll know how out of character it is for me to be writing a book in defense of the whole Bible. There are so many reasons *not* to put stock in a three-thousand-year-old religious book full of miracles and outdated rules, especially since it's been translated hundreds of times and we don't have a single original copy.

I've spent my whole life with the Bible. As a kid, I believed it because I was told that's what the best kids do. In college, I rejected it because I was told that's what the brightest students do. In my twenties, I used the parts that supported my leftist politics, and I ignored all the rest. This book is the story of how a snarky, cynical, social justice warrior came to believe that the Bible is perfect and true.

This book is the story of how a snarky, cynical, social justice warrior came to believe that the Bible is perfect and true.

I became a Christian when I was thirty-four, a full thirteen years after becoming a pastor. "How does one become a pastor without being a Christian?" I hear you asking. It was pretty simple, really.

I lied.

I grew up in rural northeast Texas, also known as the buckle of the Bible Belt. My dad is a pastor, and so were my grandfather, great-grandfather, and great-great-grandfather before him. My entire life has revolved around my small-town Methodist church, and I was the poster boy for straitlaced, cookie-cutter, red-blooded American Christianity.

Then I went off to college and married the cutest Christian girl I could find, and between my junior and senior years, I accepted the first ministry job that came my way. At twenty-one years of age, and for a salary of $16,000 a year, I became the pastor of Mooringsport Methodist Church in northern Louisiana. No one who knew me was surprised by my life's trajectory. *Goody two-shoes small-town preacher's kid gets married young and becomes a pastor* was precisely the path my friends and family had predicted for me.

But there was one problem. During the year prior, under the guidance of two particularly persuasive professors, I had come to the conclusion that Christianity was—like all other religions—a man-made construct designed to fool gullible peasants into submission by playing on their fears of death and damnation.

For the next thirteen years, I did and said what I had to in order to play the part of a pastor.

But did I truly believe in the foundational promises of God as presented in Scripture? Did I believe that the God of Israel is the one and only true God? Or that Moses actually parted the Red Sea? Or that Mary was a virgin when she gave birth to Jesus? Or that Jesus physically rose from the dead? Or that anything in the Book of Revelation makes any sense whatsoever?

Nope.

To my skeptical eyes, the Bible looked no different than any other old, religious text. I assumed it was written by religious men for the purpose of maintaining social order. Cynical to the core, I figured, *What better way to manipulate the masses than with the promise of eternal paradise as a reward for good behavior, and the threat of unrelenting hellfire for those who get out of line?*

So why would someone with such disdain for religious conformity enlist to become a clergyman? In a word, politics. As a left-leaning activist with a chip on my shoulder, I found the Bible to be a familiar and formidable weapon in the war against what I perceived to be conservative Christian bigotry. Cherry-picking verses that supported my pro-immigration, LGBTQ+ inclusion, semi-socialist views became my favorite pastime. I suppose it never occurred to me how convenient it was to leave out all the other parts—passages about personal repentance, sexual holiness, and Jesus's mandate to "make disciples of all nations." I enjoyed sarcastically reminding cranky, white evangelicals that Jesus said to love your enemies and that they're supposed to love Iraqis and gays and abortion doctors.

Of course I never stopped to consider my own hypocrisy: conservative Christians were my mortal enemies, but I felt no love for them. If I believed in hell back then, I would've told them to go there.

Internally, I was falling apart: depressed, isolated, and struggling with a porn addiction. I knew I couldn't keep living a lie forever, so I went to law school for a year and a half, until I realized that to become a big-shot lawyer you have to be even more duplicitous than a pastor with no faith. I was stuck until late 2012 when, out of nowhere, an activist friend named Andrea asked me if I had ever been to the Holy Land. When I told her that I had not, she said, "You need to see with your own eyes how the Zionists are abusing the Palestinians; I'm going to find a way to get you over there." Nine months later, thanks to Andrea and several other friends, I found myself exploring the land that gave rise to the Bible.

In Capernaum, I died. My old, divided life passed away the day I stood near the ancient house on the northern shore of the Sea of Galilee where first-generation Christians began to worship in the years following Jesus's death. My friend who was with me is an archaeology enthusiast, and he taught me how, on the walls of that ancient house-church, archaeologists discovered graffiti that reads, "God Jesus Christ" and "Christ have mercy." That part didn't surprise me; I knew Christians had been calling Jesus their "God" ever since the days of Emperor Constantine's famous Edict of Milan.

But then he said, "Those engravings have been dated to the first half of the first century AD,"[2] and my ontological foundations began to tremble beneath me. One of my favorite weapons to use against evangelical Christians was the argument that Jesus's divinity was a later amendment to the original biblical narrative. My professors insisted that upgrading Jesus from a failed apocalyptic prophet to the one true God in the flesh was nothing more than politics, the sort of power play commonly found in the history of human religions.

What does it mean, then, that this graffiti was scratched onto those walls at least two hundred sixty-three years before the Edict of Milan, not to mention decades prior to Mark writing the first Gospel? It means that the people who knew Jesus best—his friends, followers, and even his own flesh and blood—worshiped him as their God, and not just while he was alive, but even after he died on the cross.

I knew enough about Jewish scriptures and beliefs to be certain that, for any self-respecting Jew, worshiping a man was off-limits. In the Old Testament, not even Abraham, Moses, or Elijah were worthy of worship. The rule against worshiping mere men sits atop the Ten Commandments (Exodus 20:3). But the faithful Jews who walked with Jesus, some of whom watched him die, *worshiped* him and called him *God*, and many of them died for this heretical, treasonous belief.

That day in Capernaum, I was faced with history's most consequential question: *Was Jesus just a man, or is he truly God?* After weighing the evidence and searching my heart, I came to the conclusion that it is more likely than not that Jesus is who he—and his followers—said he was: Emmanuel, God with us.

For thirteen years, every time I opened that book, I expected to find something to disagree with, something to hate.

Making that decision was relatively easy; figuring out what to do about it was the tricky part. If Jesus is God, I knew I would have to revisit the Bible. For thirteen years, every time I opened that book, I expected to find something to disagree with, something to hate. But once I realized that Jesus loved the Bible, that he never criticized or contradicted it, and that he quoted it often, I knew I had more work to do. I couldn't continue calling Jesus my God while feeling such animosity toward his Word.

So here I am, the most cynical person I know, writing a book defending the book I once loved to hate. And I won't just be defending the good parts, either. Anyone can appreciate the *Good Samaritan* and the *Golden Rule*, but how can any decent, thinking person make sense of the violent, genocidal, misogynistic, homophobic, pro-slavery sections of Scripture?

That question is what motivated me to write this book.

So let's get started.

CHAPTER ONE

ISN'T THE BIBLE ONLY HUMAN?

For people destined to inherit paradise in heaven for all eternity, Christians can be such fragile little snowflakes sometimes. Every other day, it seems like another group of believers gets triggered over some new, imminent threat to their faith. In my lifetime I've seen Christians express outrage over everything from dancing teenagers and Super Bowl halftime shows to men in skinny jeans and women in yoga pants. Just this morning, my Twitter feed informed me that thousands of Southern Baptists are up in arms because a woman was invited to a Baptist conference to offer a spoken word performance during a worship service.

A *woman*, you guys!

The trouble with this particular woman is that she describes herself as a pastor which, for most Southern Baptists, is unacceptable because there are verses in the New Testament forbidding women to lead or teach Christian men. I'm not arguing in favor of female pastors here (I'll do that later in the book); right now, my point is simply that this woman wasn't even invited to preach or teach at that Baptist conference; she was simply asked to recite some cool poetry she wrote. Still, a mob of Christians is threatening to boycott the event because this pastor and her poetry pose a clear and present danger to their biblical purity.

I don't mean to attack anyone's doctrine here; I know that most Christians who believe women shouldn't be pastors are just doing their best to be obedient to Scripture. But when I read about stories like this woman and her spoken word performance evoking such a negative, public response from Christians, I wonder if we have forgotten the words of Jesus who, after his disciples tried to stop a stranger from doing good things in Jesus's name, said, "'Do not stop him.'... 'For whoever is not against us is for us'" (Mark 9:39-40). The advice of the apostle Peter applies here as well:

> But in your hearts revere Christ as Lord. Always be
> prepared to give an answer to everyone who asks you to
> give the reason for the hope that you have. But do this with
> gentleness and respect. (1 Peter 3:15, emphasis added)

Christians tend to have a pretty good handle on "Always be prepared to give an answer," but we're often deficient in the "with gentleness and respect" department. Insecurity is what I see when I observe how some Christians interact with the wider culture, which begs the question: If our tickets to heaven are already punched, why are many Christians so insecure?

Baptist theology

I've concluded that the driver of Christian insecurity is a deep fear many believers experience when we don't have what it takes to defend the Bible in our twenty-first-century secular context. Our fragility stems from the burden we feel to read, obey, honor, and defend a book that most of us have not been trained to interpret. Despite our lack of preparation, we feel obligated to protect the Bible, so whenever a threat to our holy book emerges, the claws come out.

And how do you protect something you don't fully understand? How do you defend a book when your opponents publicly point out the verses that appear archaic at best, and morally indefensible at worst? You fight. You get angry. You regurgitate something you heard your preacher say. You make your point, and if your opponents refuse to accept it, the "Unfriend" button is just a click away.

Creepy Uncle Cain

I was in high school the first time I remember seeing Christian insecurity about the Bible on full display. Even though my dad was the pastor at the Methodist church in town, I preferred the non-denominational church's youth group because of the ~~organized structure and in-depth Bible teaching~~ basketball court. Plus, the non-denom girls were way cuter. One night, the church's youth minister, Greg, decided to teach us about the story of Cain and Abel who, in addition to being the sons of Adam and Eve, were also the world's first murderer and murder victim, respectively. After telling us how Cain slaughtered his little brother and then proceeded to get snarky with God about it (God: "Where is your brother Abel?"

Cain: "I don't know. *Am I my brother's keeper?*"), Youth Pastor Greg dropped this confounding verse on us: "Cain made love to his wife…" (Genesis 4:17).

I could see the terror in Youth Pastor Greg's face the moment he stopped reading. He had to be kicking himself for saying that final verse out loud. He never intended for his lesson on Genesis 4 to take the unfortunate turn that suddenly felt inevitable. Predictably, a sophomore raised her hand and asked the question on most of our minds, "Where did Cain's wife come from?"

In case you're unfamiliar with the problem presented by Cain's wife, here it is: In Genesis 1, God made two people, Adam and Eve. In the next chapter, they married each other (not a very deep dating pool!). In chapter 3, they ate one bad apple and all hell broke loose. God forced them to leave the Garden of Eden. In the fourth chapter, they made love and had kids. At this point in the story, if you read the text literally, Adam and Eve's nuclear family were the only people on the planet, so the obvious answer to the sophomore's question is that Cain married his own sister which, to a roomful of adolescents like us, sounded both horrendous and hilarious.

The noise of chaos and laughter swelled in the Youth Room. Whatever lesson Youth Pastor Greg intended to teach was a moot point. He downshifted into damage control because the only talking point that we students were taking home that night was the apparent incest in Genesis 4. Trying to think on his feet, and perhaps clinging to his job, Youth Pastor Greg insisted we were wrong. He said, "It's impossible that God would allow Cain to marry his sister because Leviticus 18 says marrying your sister is a sin. The Bible forbids it, so it could not have happened."

The sophomore's boyfriend interrupted: "But doesn't the Bible forbid murder, too? *That* happened. Ask Abel!" Youth Pastor Greg pretended not to hear him.

Then someone shouted, "So who *was* Cain's wife?!" All sweaty, Youth Pastor Greg explained, "What must have happened is that Adam and Eve had other kids, and then their kids had kids, and after enough time passed, Cain married one of them."

"Wait," the sophomore shot back, "So Cain married his *niece*?"

A collective "Ewwwwwww" spread like a virus across the room, as the thought of marrying an uncle or aunt caused each of us to upchuck in our mouths a little. Knowing he had no chance of gaining control over that room again, Youth Pastor Greg shouted, "If I let you go play basketball, will you promise not to tell your parents what happened here tonight?" We accepted his terms of surrender.

The controversy over whom Cain married is indicative of a much larger question that is tearing Christians, churches, and denominations apart: How should we respond when someone challenges our Scriptures, especially when the Bible appears ambiguous about the issues being raised? Absent some better answer, the typical Christian counter to tough questions about the Bible is to get defensive, which rarely produces a fruitful exchange with skeptics. If anything, the Christian tendency toward panicked, circular logic pushes intelligent doubters even further away from faith in God.

My Brother's Keeper?

What are we so afraid of? Do we really think the book with a two-thousand-year shelf life and the number-one best seller in history can't take a little heat from modern intellectuals? Are we really so afraid that a few questions from unbelievers could cause the entire canon to crumble unless we quickly offer a foolproof defense? Wouldn't that imply that the Bible is nothing but a house of cards anyway? We don't think so little of this book, do we? Of course not.

We don't need to jump through hoops to explain away uncomfortable questions about Cain's wife. Consider this much simpler, more reasonable line of reasoning: (1) the first few chapters in Genesis are not an eyewitness report, (2) it doesn't really matter whom Cain married, and (3) the only thing that matters in this story is God's love for Cain.

Central to the story is the fact that Cain was the world's premier homicidal maniac, and that God loved him nonetheless. Before killing his brother, "Cain was very angry, and his face was downcast" (Genesis 4:5). God, aware of Cain's toxic resentment, tried to warn the young man:

> "Why are you angry? Why is your face downcast? If you
> do what is right, will you not be accepted? But if you do not
> do what is right, sin is crouching at your door; it desires to
> have you, but you must rule over it." (Genesis 4:6-7)

Cain did not rule over it. Instead, he invited his brother to go on a walk, and later that day, Cain walked back home, alone. Fully aware of what Cain had done, God gave the man a chance to confess:

> "Where is your brother Abel?"
>
> "I don't know," he replied. "Am I my brother's keeper?"
>
> The LORD said, "What have you done?" (Genesis 4:9-10)

Many Christians and non-Christians alike have absorbed the supposition that "Old Testament God" was meaner and morally inferior when compared to "New Testament God."

Even if you've never read the Bible, you've likely heard about God's reputation for wrath and bloodthirst in the Old Testament. Many Christians and non-Christians alike have absorbed the supposition that "Old Testament God" was meaner and morally inferior when compared to "New Testament God," who was the embodiment of mercy and love. How, then, would you expect *mean old God* to react to Cain's monstrous sin? With an equally monstrous penalty, right? If ever a man was deserving of capital punishment, it was Cain.

But *mean old God* is full of surprises. For the crime of murder in the first degree, God sentenced Cain to a life of hunting and gathering instead of farming:

> *"When you work the ground, it will no longer yield its crops for you. You will be a restless wanderer on the earth."* (Genesis 4:12)

That's it! So much for the bloodthirsty God of the Old Testament. Still, instead of jumping for joy, Cain aired his grievances:

> *"My punishment is more than I can bear. Today you are driving me from the land, and I will be hidden from your presence. I will be a restless wanderer on the earth, and whoever finds me will kill me."* (Genesis 4:13-14)

After receiving the lightest possible sentence for the worst imaginable crime, Cain had the hubris to play the victim. To be clear, if I was God, those might have been Cain's last words. *Are you kidding me, Cain? Who do you think you are?* But how did God respond to Cain's fear of being killed?

> *"Not so; anyone who kills Cain will suffer vengeance seven times over." Then the LORD put a mark on Cain so that no one who found him would kill him. So Cain went out from the LORD's presence and lived in the land of Nod, east of Eden.* (Genesis 4:15-16)

Wait, *what?* "Old Testament God" promised to protect the world's first murderer? Why? Because all along, throughout the entire story, God was answering Cain's question. The same question the people of God continued to ask in all sixty-six books of the Bible. It's the question Jesus came to answer once and for all. And in this age of movements like Black Lives Matter, #MeToo, and the battle over abortion rights, this question looms large even now.

"Am I my brother's keeper?" asked Cain. In other words:

Am I responsible for what I do?

Am I expected to protect the most vulnerable?

Am I made to love?

And God, merciful and kind, looked at Cain the murderer and said, "*Yes you are.*"

The Humanity of the Bible

Understood in a vacuum, Cain's story is an interesting fable about being nice to your siblings, but in the greater context of the Bible,

Cain's failures and God's forgiveness foreshadow future events. Like much of the Old Testament, the story of Cain and Abel has no satisfying end; it beckons us to anticipate someone better than Cain and something better than sin.

The Old Testament is amazing on its own, but as a prequel to the life of Jesus, it's epic. Everything you find in the Old Testament—even the awful, ugly parts—points forward to the life of Jesus. The humanity on display in the Hebrew Scriptures is both repulsive and redemptive. Take Abraham, for example; by all accounts, the father of Judaism, Christianity, and Islam was a man of great faith. We're introduced to Abraham (who was also called Abram) in Genesis, the first book of the Bible:

> The LORD had said to Abram, "Go from your country, your people and your father's household to the land I will show you.
>
> "I will make you into a great nation; . . .
> I will make your name great. . . .
> And all peoples on earth
> will be blessed through you."
>
> So Abram went. . . . (Genesis 12:1-4)

Wow! Abram had a comfortable life, and just walked away because God told him to. What a godly man of faith, right? One day, I hope to become half the man that Abr—*OK, hold that thought.* Six verses later, Abraham traveled with Sarai to Egypt to escape a famine, and before crossing the border, it occurred to Abraham that his wife was gorgeous:

> *As he was about to enter Egypt, he said to his wife Sarai,*
> *"I know what a beautiful woman you are. When the*
> *Egyptians see you, they will say, 'This is his wife.'" (Genesis*
> *12:11-12)*

That's really sweet. Isn't that the kind of thing every wife likes to hear? Abraham should have stopped right there, but he kept talking:

> *"Then they will kill me but will let you live. Say you are my*
> *sister, so that I will be treated well for your sake and my life*
> *will be spared because of you." (Genesis 12:12-13)*

Yikes. That's slightly less romantic. The story only gets worse from there. As Abraham predicted, Egyptian men took note of Sarai's beauty, and when Pharaoh heard about her,

> *she was taken into his palace. He treated Abram well for*
> *her sake, and Abram acquired sheep and cattle, male and*
> *female donkeys, male and female servants, and camels.*
> *(Genesis 12:15-16)*

In case you didn't catch that, mere moments after his courageous response to God's call, Abraham swapped his wife's dignity to protect himself. As he laid eyes on all his new livestock and servants, Pharaoh laid eyes on Abraham's "sister," and just so we're clear, "she was taken into his palace" was Egyptian for "Pharaoh wanted to *Netflix and chill.*"

So wait—was Abraham a good guy, or a bad guy? Was he faithful, or flawed?

He was both, and the same can be said for most of the other key figures in the Bible. Moses was a murderer, Sarai abused her servant, Rebekah was deceptive, Samson was the Jewish Hulk, David used his power to sexually possess another man's wife (and then he had the man killed), and Peter was a coward. *To err is human*, the old adage goes. Universally, screwing up is what it *means* to be a human being.

Well, *almost* universally.

The Bible is a collection of many stories about many imperfect people, but at its core we find the story of the only perfect Person. The legitimacy of Scripture hangs on the perfection of Jesus. For skeptics, this begs the question: *What do Christians mean when we say Jesus was perfect?*

Some have said that Jesus is perfect because he is God, and while we believe that to be true, we shouldn't miss the point that Jesus was perfectly human, too. In our rush to worship his divinity, it can be so easy to forget that Jesus was, for a time, *a guy*. No halo, no white robe, and no dreamy blue eyes gazing thoughtfully into the distance. He was just a regular, first-century Jewish man from the sticks, and he did all the things regular, first-century country boys did: he worked in construction, spent time with his buddies, drank a little, and looked after his mama.

So where are all the paintings of Jesus just being a guy? Where's the oil-on-canvas of my Lord and Savior looking under his bed for the matching sock? Or the sculpture of Christ popping a zit in front of his mirror? Or the Renaissance portrait of the Son of Man smashing his thumb with a hammer? Those pieces don't exist, perhaps because it's not easy to conceive of Jesus's humanity.

It wasn't easy for Jesus, either. On several occasions, the four biographies of Jesus in the New Testament (called *Matthew, Mark, Luke,* and *John*) give us intimate glimpses of his struggle to come to terms with human limitations. Matthew's memoir recounts the time he asked his buddies what people were saying about him behind his back. His friends went easy on him; they didn't mention all the rumors that were flying around—that he was a heretic (John 10:33) and a drunk (Luke 7:34) who believed that sex-workers were more deserving of heaven than religious leaders (Matthew 21:31). They told him some people thought he was a great teacher, while others called him a prophet. Then Jesus asked his friends what *they* thought about him (Matthew 16:15).

Why on earth would Jesus care what anybody thinks about him? He's *Jesus,* you know? All-powerful and stuff. Was he really doubting his own identity? I doubt it; he knew who he was. Was he just testing his disciples? Perhaps. But I think it's also possible that Jesus wanted to know what people were saying about him because he was a human being, and all human beings want to know what people think about us. That's why your glands release dopamine when somebody likes your Instagram selfie. That's why we google ourselves. That's why some people hack into their ex's email to see what she's been writing about you.

You know who you are.

Can you imagine what it must have been like for the eternal Creator to become one of us? Or how strange it must have been for God to feel hunger for the first time? Or to need a nap? Or to smash his thumb with a hammer or to catch feelings for a girl or to be insecure and wonder what people are saying about him?

Ever since he asked, "Who do they say that I am?" people in every time and place have been repeating the same question: "Who is Jesus?" Is he truly God, just a great prophet, or something else? How we understand the Bible depends entirely on this question.

Who Was Jesus?

To answer this question, we have to take a closer look at the accounts of those who knew Jesus personally. In this chapter, I'll offer some of the evidence that led me and many others to believe that the four memoirs of Jesus's life were very likely penned by two of his own disciples (Matthew and John), the interpreter for his lead disciple, Simon Peter (Mark), and the only non-Jewish biblical author (Luke) who may not have known Jesus personally but who knew many of the people in Jesus's inner circle.

For thirty-plus years, most people thought Jesus was just a bright, small-town bachelor whose faith and heritage were important to him. Jesus knew the Hebrew Bible[1] and observed the laws and traditions that were sacred to his people. He wasn't exactly an altar boy, though; remember, his worst enemies were priests and preachers.

What did Jesus look like? No one knows for sure, although I think it's safe to say that a first-century Middle Eastern Jew didn't resemble most of the portraits we've all seen of him in famous works of art.

The most likely answer is that Jesus was average looking. Why? Because when somebody is not average looking, we describe them using their extraordinary features, but if someone doesn't have any remarkable physical features, you have to find other ways to talk about them. How would you describe the most physically average guy you know to your friends? You wouldn't mention his facial features or his body type, would you? Be honest: you probably don't even remember anything about his appearance because he's so physically forgettable. Instead, you'd mention something he did or said, right?

When the New Testament authors described Jesus, they did so using his words and actions instead of his physical attributes—which is really interesting because, throughout the rest of the Bible, authors are quick to point out other people's distinguishing features. When describing David, for example, the Hebrew prophet Samuel said, "He was glowing with health and had a fine appearance and handsome features" (1 Samuel 16:12). The Book of Genesis describes Joseph as "well-built and handsome" (Genesis 39:6), Moses was "beautiful" (Hebrews 11:23 ESV), Sarai was hot (Genesis 12:14), Samson was ripped (Judges 16:3-5), Goliath was tall (1 Samuel 17:4). There is precedent in Scripture for describing what the main characters looked like, but the New Testament writers left no clues about the appearance of the most important man in the Bible. Why? Perhaps because, physically speaking, Jesus was perfectly average.

Thanks to archaeologists and anthropologists, we have a fairly good idea what average Galilean men looked like in the first century.

Archaeological records suggest Jesus probably stood around 5'5" with olive skin, coarse hair, and large, deep-set eyes.[2] We can also make assumptions based on Jesus's line of work. You've probably heard that, like his father before him, Jesus was a "carpenter," but that word lacks precision. We should be careful not to glamorize his career as though he had his own private woodshop, fully stocked with blueprints, table saws, and stacks of spare lumber lying around.

The Bible authors refer to Joseph and Jesus as *tektons* (Mark 6:3; Matthew 13:55), a title that was typically given to hard-working day-laborers in the construction business. By contrast, they were not called *arki-tektons*, the proper title for highly trained, professional master-craftsmen. In Jesus's world, being a *tekton* wasn't a very noble profession; on the ladder of success, *tektons* were one rung below farmers, and one rung above beggars. The disrespect that some elites harbored for a mere *tekton* like Jesus was on full display after he became a rabbi and went to teach in Nazareth, his hometown. He was such a gifted, authoritative teacher that he made the religious leaders jealous, so they said: "Isn't this the *tekton's* son?" (from Matthew 13:55).

To be clear: those Nazarene rabbis didn't forget Joseph's name. Nazareth was a small town of less than three hundred people; they knew Jesus's dad very well. This was not an honest inquiry; "Isn't this big shot the son of a *tekton*?" was an insult.

Whenever you think of Jesus, you should probably think less "tall, fair, and skinny" and more "workhorse with a strong back standing outside of Home Depot on a Monday morning, hoping to find work." Men like Jesus had to grind to scratch out a living. Lucky for him, around the time he was growing up, the Roman government funded the restoration of a massive city called Sepphoris, about six miles from his home in Nazareth. Between his childhood and the inception of his ministry, it is possible that Jesus was working alongside his father and younger brothers in Sepphoris, fulfilling his duty as Joseph's firstborn son.

When he was about thirty, Jesus left his construction job to launch his movement. But do you think two decades of walking twelve miles round-trip, six days a week, while carrying his tools to arrive at a construction site where he lifted bricks and swung a hammer for twelve hours a day, left Jesus looking frail and pale? No way. Five-foot-five, olive-skinned, hairy Jesus was a certified alpha dog. He was the kind of man that even the strongest men died to follow. He spent most of his adult life laying foundations, building a city, and making something out of nothing. Then, in the last few years of his life, Jesus applied those *tekton* skills to his ministry of building up people.

According to the Gospel writers, most of his closest friends and family didn't seem to understand who Jesus was until the very end of his life, while others were not convinced of his true identity until after his death and resurrection (Mark 3:20-21, John 7:5). For some, even his resurrection was not enough to dispel their doubts. Matthew tells us that after Jesus died and rose from the grave, he spent forty days with his disciples, preparing them for life without him. Then, when the time came for Jesus to leave, Matthew says the disciples began to worship him, "but some doubted" (Matthew 28:17). Even then, some weren't sure who Jesus was.

The authors of Matthew, Mark, Luke, and John wrote to give an answer to the world's most consequential question. Whether they were right or wrong about Jesus, they *believed* they were recording history. They weren't updating some old myth about an ancient, fictional hero. They *knew* him, touched him, smelled him, lived with him, ate and drank with him, and many of them left their day jobs to follow him.

When Jesus's life on earth was over, these men realized that he came to undo what Cain had done. Cain tore his brother down; Jesus lifted his people up. Cain said, "Am I my brother's keeper?" Jesus answered Cain's question with a story about a prodigal son, his brother who despised him, and their loving father's desire to reconcile them to one another.

Most people know that Jesus came to reveal the face of true divinity, but so few of us understand that he also came to restore something that Cain lost long ago: *the perfect heart of true humanity.*

The Perfection We Need

Perhaps that's little consolation if you've put your stock in biblical Christianity before, only to be left disappointed or heartbroken by judgmental believers with Bibles in their hands. It really shouldn't surprise us, however, when hypocrites are drawn to God's word; hypocrites are his target audience! May we never forget that the most important character in the Bible was judged to death by religious people quoting the scriptures. Only God could inspire a book that is so revered by the same people it most harshly condemns; it's a master class in irony!

Because religion and religious leaders fall so far short of the glory of Jesus and his gospel, most skeptics are left to assume that the Bible is an imperfect book written for people who think they're perfect. When you learn to distinguish between religions of men and the gospel of Jesus, it's clear: the Bible is the perfect book for people who know they're flawed.

The most important difference between man-made religion and God-inspired gospel is probably shame. Religion is designed to trap people in cycles of shame over their sin. You mess up, you think you're going to hell, you go to your preferred house of worship, you pay your dues, you feel a little better about yourself, until you mess up again…and the cycle continues.

> *Historically speaking, religions have*
> *capitalized on our shame, but Jesus never did.*
> *He canceled it instead.*

Obviously, I'm oversimplifying religion, but I am just so tired of hearing Christians conflating man-made religion with the gospel of Jesus Christ. Historically speaking, religions have capitalized on our shame, but Jesus never did. He canceled it instead. Why, then, do so many Christians continue to live in shame and fear instead of embracing the freedom of Jesus? And why, when we attempt to share the gospel with the world, do we so often begin the story with our sin, instead of with the goodness of God and how he created human beings in his image? As Alan Hirsch has written:

> So often [evangelical Christianity] falls into the trap of starting its proclamation of the gospel in Genesis 3 (original sin) rather than in Genesis 1 (original blessing). When this happens, the good news simply becomes about how we get rid of all that guilt and all that sin. But…if we reduce the gospel by beginning with the problem, then the whole search for God becomes a negative problem-solving journey. And to those who are desperately searching for something more, reducing the good news to problem-solving and moralism presents itself as an exercise in futility.[3]

The Bible is so much more than just a negative problem-solving journey! It is the story of a perfect God who created every human being in his image, and even though we've rebelled against his perfect will for us, he will stop at nothing to rescue us from the consequences of our sin and to restore us to his image. That's a *good* story, and it's infinitely better than anything religion has to offer.

Even if you've never been blacklisted by Bible-thumpers, you still may find the Christian holy book to be confusing and off-putting. When taken at face value, the Bible offers skeptical readers plenty of reasons to walk away, scratching their heads. Take this little nugget from the Old Testament book of Deuteronomy:

> *If two men are fighting and the wife of one of them comes to rescue her husband from his assailant, and she reaches out and seizes him by his private parts, you shall cut off her hand. Show her no pity. (Deuteronomy 25:11-12)*

Just to be clear, I've given my wife permission to do whatever is necessary to help me survive a fight. Why in the world would the Word of God call for such a savvy wife to lose her hand? Incidentally, my favorite translation of this passage is the King James version, which awkwardly reads:

> *When men strive together one with another, and the wife of the one draweth near for to deliver her husband out of the hand of him that smiteth him, and putteth forth her hand, and* taketh him by the secrets:
>
> *Then thou shalt cut off her hand…. (Deuteronomy 25:11-12 KJV, emphasis added)*

Taketh him by the secrets?!

For many skeptics and freethinkers, it's nearly impossible to believe that the one true God would endorse a book containing comically outmoded passages like these, but this is why biblical literacy is so important. When you understand how to read the Bible, it comes as no surprise that its narrative can occasionally be ridiculous, temperamental, and lacking in detail. After all, it was penned by human beings—real people who had real pain, problems, and limitations.

Perfect God + Imperfect People = The Perfect Story

Christians believe the people who wrote the Bible were inspired by God; in fact, we think every word of Scripture is "God-breathed" (2 Timothy 3:16). That does not mean, however, that we believe the entire Bible fell from heaven as a finished product in the King's English, gilded pages and all. It means that God inspired all the stories, laws, songs, and prophecies that make up our Scriptures as they were being written, and he still inspires them now as they are being read.

The divine inspiration of Scripture does not preclude the fact that God's perfect message for the world passed through human filters. You can't read the Bible without seeing its raw humanity; the sporadic examples of textual discrepancies, the occasional shocking misogyny, and the examples of extreme violence leap off its pages. This undeniable fact terrifies biblically insecure Christians, but we should never see the humanity of Scripture as a threat to its veracity.

The question is not whether the human element sullies the original Word of God; instead, we should be asking, "Does the humanity of Scripture damage its integrity?"

I don't believe it does. Before I became a Christian, I used what I thought were flaws in the Bible to poke holes in the Truth claims that Christians hold dear. I would question, for example, why the four Gospel writers disagree on the order of events in Jesus's life. Did Jesus famously turn over the tables in the Temple toward the end of his life, as Matthew and Mark suggest, or was it at the very beginning of his ministry, like John says? Luke says there were two angels in Jesus's tomb on Easter morning. Matthew and Mark say there was one. And John, the only Gospel writer who was actually *at* Jesus's tomb on Easter morning, didn't mention the presence of any angels at all.

I used to think these obvious discrepancies represented the proverbial nail in the coffin for the Bible. No thinking person could ever accept this internally inconsistent collection of ancient books as authoritative or divinely inspired, right?

It's just not that simple. Once my life changed in Capernaum, I began to revisit some of my deepest doubts about the Bible, and I felt compelled to start asking better questions. Instead of "Why would a perfect God write such an imperfect book?" I started asking, "If the standard of biblical truth was the absolute absence of discrepancies, why didn't the early Christians ever 'clean up' the scriptures?" Generations of believers had plenty of opportunities to dispose of the minor discrepancies within the Gospel stories with some careful editing, so why didn't they take advantage?

Maybe worshiping a perfect book was never the point for Christians because, while the Bible's inerrancy makes for fiery conversations and controversial books, we know that a holy book—perfect though it may be—can never save a single soul because a book can't show us how to live. Only a person can do that.

The Bible is the story of the only perfect human. The lack of discrepancies and minor historical flaws isn't what makes the Bible perfect; the Bible is perfect because of Jesus: God's perfect gift for this imperfect world.

It's the Bible's humanity that speaks to my skeptical heart. Any holy book claiming to be anything other than human-filtered is a fraud from the start. It's not the human element, but the supposed lack of it, that negates the sacredness of any so-called sacred text. Anything short of a humanized holy book is mere magic, the stuff of fairy tales we tell restless children until they finally give up and go to sleep, or worse: the stuff of false religions we preach to restless adults until they do.

The only Bible worth believing is God-breathed and human-filtered.

The only God worth trusting is the Son of Man.

The message that matters most is God's love for all humanity.

For women pastors and the people who judge them.

And thoughtful wives who taketh an attacker by the *secrets*.

For Cain.

And Youth Pastor Greg.

Even for me.

Even for you.

CHAPTER TWO

IS THE BIBLE
FACT OR FICTION?

Christians believe that God inspired the Bible, but he didn't write it. Flawed human beings actually wrote it, and then some other flawed humans collected and compiled the sixty-six–book anthology we call the Bible. For many skeptics, that's reason enough to walk away from the Bible and never look back. Waking up to the *humanity* of those responsible for producing the Bible, including what I perceived to be their unforgivable sins—misogyny, approval of slavery, and backward sexual ethics—was the first step along my path to disbelief in my twenties.

If that wasn't enough to open my eyes to the irrational nature of Christianity's claims about biblical authority, I later learned about something called the *oral tradition*. Not only was the Bible written by some dubious characters, but most of it was written decades, if not centuries, after the events in question took place. Reports of these events were passed down for generations by word of mouth before they were ever written down. If we are honest about human nature, we know that people are prone to embellishment when it comes to the stories we love.

Do you remember playing the "telephone" game when you were a kid? It's the one where kids sit in a circle and take turns whispering a phrase into each other's ears—something innocuous, like "On Sundays we have donuts for breakfast." But by the time the phrase makes its way around the circle, the last kid hears something like "Some days your mom drinks beer for breakfast," which would be vastly more concerning than eating donuts for breakfast once a week.

Is that what happened with the Bible? Even if we say the stories were true in their original form, isn't it safe to assume they were corrupted over time through oral tradition and the compilation process, not to mention the many translations they have undergone?

In other words, is there any way for an honest skeptic to accept the Bible as true, especially when it bears all the classic marks of mythology?

Pickups and Subarus

I once spent an entire day asking random people on the streets of downtown Houston whether they believed the Bible is fact or fiction. You might think everyone said "fact" because you've heard that Houston is a homogeneous Bible Belt city, but H-town is actually the most diverse city in the United States.[1] The inner city where I live is overwhelmingly secular.

The results of my sidewalk survey were revealing: around 40 percent of the people I approached said the Bible is fiction, another 40 percent said it's fact, and nearly 20 percent responded with some version of "Who are you? Leave me alone, sir. Don't make me call the cops." Another observation: 90 percent of men in pickup trucks said the Bible is *fact*, while 90 percent of women in Subarus swore that it is *fiction*.

Meanwhile, the lion's share of us keep to ourselves because we're afraid of being berated by extremists on either side.

Truth be told, most people think the Bible sits somewhere on the spectrum between fiction and fact. I think of it like a bell curve, where a small minority of people (the crazy irrational Left) are convinced the Bible is absolutely fictional, while another minority of people (the crazy irrational Right) are certain the Bible is entirely factual. Meanwhile, the lion's share of us keep to ourselves because we're afraid of being berated by extremists on either side.

No matter how you answer it, you inevitably run into problems.

Those who say the Bible is fiction must explain the many accurate accounts of historical events throughout both the Old and New Testaments. Being a naysayer is easy; I've done it most of my adult life. Anybody can claim to discredit the Bible by quoting a verse here or a passage there and pulling it out of context to invalidate it, but stopping there would be lazy and irresponsible, and I know you're not lazy and irresponsible because you're reading a book, and only

41

the smartest people still read books in the twenty-first century. So let's take a closer look at the source material.

For centuries, scholars believed most of the events described in the Old Testament were exaggerated, if not entirely mythical; with each passing year, however, archaeologists are uncovering ancient artifacts that create real problems for those who love to discredit the Bible. In spite of what you may have heard, the thirty-nine books of the Old Testament describe many ancient, factual events with unrivaled accuracy. Here are a few examples:

THE MERNEPTAH STELE

Left-leaning Bible scholars used to say that the tribe or nation called Israel didn't exist until after 1000 BC, which would suggest that the events described in the Bible prior to that time—Genesis through 1 Samuel, more or less—were either purely fictional, or the accounts were borrowed from other, foreign tribes and nations. That idea was dealt a major blow in 1896 when, among the ruins of ancient Thebes on the west bank of the Nile River, British Egyptologist Flinders Petrie unearthed an artifact that disrupted the widely accepted narrative supporting biblical mythology.

The Merneptah Stele dates all the way back to around 1230 BC, and on it, the Egyptian Pharaoh Merneptah refers to Israel as a rival tribe.[2] If, by that time, the people called Israel were already established enough to be recognized, and called by name, by neighboring monarchs of larger empires, Israel surely existed for many generations prior to 1230. Contrary to the *settled science* of academic historians, Israel certainly did exist long before 1000 BC, just as the Bible said they did.

KING HEZEKIAH'S TUNNEL

Two Old Testament books—2 Kings and 2 Chronicles—make the claim that, when the kingdom of Judah was under attack by the Assyrians in the seventh century BC, King Hezekiah heroically saved the capital city of Jerusalem by ordering the construction of a massive underground tunnel that provided fresh water to the city's embattled citizens.

> *When Hezekiah saw that Sennacherib had come and that he intended to wage war against Jerusalem, he consulted with his officials and military staff about blocking off the water from the springs outside the city, and they helped him. They gathered a large group of people who blocked all the springs and the stream that flowed through the land. "Why should the kings of Assyria come and find plenty of water?" they said. (2 Chronicles 32:2-4)*

> *As for the other events of Hezekiah's reign, all his achievements and how he made the pool and the tunnel by which he brought water into the city, are they not written in the book of the annals of the kings of Judah? (2 Kings 20:20)*

Secular historians called it just another legend—a typical *big fish* story in which the details are exaggerated to make the hero look better than he actually was. Then archaeologists found the tunnel in 1838, and it was every bit as extraordinary as advertised in the Bible. In 1880 a teenager went for a swim through the tunnel and found an inscription left by the men who built it. To the surprise of many, historians dated the inscription to the time of King Hezekiah's reign.[3]

43

THE CYRUS CYLINDER

The Old Testament books of Ezra and Nehemiah make the unusual claim that, when the Persian Empire conquered the Babylonians, King Cyrus of Persia declared freedom for the Israelites who had been forced into exile for over fifty years by Babylonian King Nebuchadnezzar:

> In the first year of Cyrus king of Persia, in order to fulfill the word of the LORD spoken by Jeremiah, the LORD moved the heart of Cyrus king of Persia to make a proclamation throughout his realm and also to put it in writing:
>
> "This is what Cyrus king of Persia says:
>
> "'The LORD, the God of heaven, has given me all the kingdoms of the earth and he has appointed me to build a temple for him at Jerusalem in Judah. Any of his people among you may go up to Jerusalem in Judah and build the temple of the LORD, the God of Israel, the God who is in Jerusalem, and may their God be with them.'" (Ezra 1:1-3)

I remember hearing my college and seminary professors scoff at the suggestion that this event ever happened because kings of ancient empires weren't known for random acts of kindness such as freeing foreign exiles. But in 1879, among the ruins of a Mesopotamian pagan temple, an archaeologist named Hormuzd Rassam came across an artifact called the Cyrus Cylinder.[4]

Historians have dated the cylinder to around 540 BC, just around the time when Ezra and Nehemiah claimed that Cyrus the

Great allowed the Hebrew exiles to go home. Among the lines he inscribed on the cylinder are these words which refer to the exiles taken captive under Babylon:

> ...whose sanctuaries had been abandoned for a long time, I returned the images of the gods, who had resided [in Babylon], to their places and I let them dwell in eternal abodes. I gathered all their inhabitants and returned to them their dwellings.[5]

Given these examples of the Bible's historical merit, and the many others that are referenced in Scripture, the oral tradition passes the smell test. To claim this book is fiction is either lazy or dishonest. The Bible contains too many facts to be mere fiction. But does the presence of facts make the Bible *fact*? Not necessarily.

Fictional Truth and Factual Lies

While the Bible actually does contain such facts, no amount of facts could possibly contain the Bible.

In addition to facts and rules for better living, the Bible has a story to tell. Some parts of the Scriptures are fiction, and that's intentional. I believe most of the first eleven chapters of Genesis, while vaguely describing historical events, were meant to be read like theological parables. The Old Testament book of Hosea clearly tells a fictional story for a theological purpose. Jesus taught using dozens of made-up stories. Nearly a third of the Bible is artistic writing: music and poetry. Musicians and poets don't typically write mere facts; they use their creative imaginations to paint pictures with words.

I know how nervous some Christians get when we start calling parts of the Bible fiction. Conceding this point seems to make the Bible susceptible to arguments from skeptics like the renowned atheist Richard Dawkins:

> "The Bible should be taught, but emphatically not as reality. It is fiction, myth, poetry, anything but reality. As such it needs to be taught because it underlies so much of our literature and our culture."[6]

I'm not sure which is more pretentious: Dawkins's casual implication that there is nothing factual about the Bible, or the elitist idea that fiction, myth, and poetry are "anything but reality." After all, the greatest works of fiction tell us more about reality than any academic journal ever could. Poetry and songs can move people in ways that empirical data cannot. Some made-up stories are deeply true, while some true stories are blatantly false.

A few years ago I watched a Martin Scorsese movie called *The Wolf of Wall Street*,[7] after which I needed to take a nice, long shower. It's the story of Jordan Belfort, who did horrible things that harmed thousands of innocent people, and when he finally got caught red-handed, his punishment was a joke. This guy stole around $200,000,000 from ordinary folks, and he served only twenty-two months in jail. Then, just before the credits rolled, these words flashed across the big screen, "Based on a True Story."

The Wolf of Wall Street might have been based on historical events, but there was nothing *true* about the story that a man can live for money, lie to his investors, cheat on his wives, abuse controlled narcotics, and steal millions of dollars, all without facing any real consequences. It might be factual, but it can't be *true*. It is the historically accurate account of an incredibly false person who amassed a false fortune by falsely claiming to care about his clients and employees when, in truth, the only person he ever loved was himself.

Compare *The Wolf of Wall Street* with the story Jesus told about a man who was approached by some thugs who beat him up, stripped him naked, and left him for dead on the side of the road. Moments later, a preacher stumbled upon the scene of the crime and saw the man lying there, half-dead. Instead of stopping to help, the preacher acted like he was in a hurry and kept walking. *There's no time to help the dying when the church service is about to start!* Then a politician walked by and did the same thing. *Dead men don't vote.*

Next, the plot thickens, as a Samaritan man happens upon the helpless victim. He pours expensive oil and wine on the man's wounds to soothe and disinfect them. He tears his own clothes and uses the strips of fabric as bandages. He picks up the man's limp, naked body and takes him to the nearest motel, where he pays for a room and nurses his wounds all night. The next morning, the man asks the hotel manager to allow the wounded victim to stay in the room for as long as necessary, and he leaves his credit card information so the hotel can charge him for whatever is owed (paraphrasing Jesus in Luke 10:25-37).

It's hard for us to imagine how shocking the idea of a "good Samaritan" was for Jesus's followers, to whom Samaritans represented everything that was wrong with the world. The Jewish-Samaritan rift went back more than seven hundred years and had escalated during Jesus's lifetime. Around the time of his birth, a group of Samaritans broke into the Jerusalem Temple and attempted to desecrate Judaism's holiest place by scattering the bones of the dead inside.[8]

But in the story Jesus told, it was the Samaritan who saved the day. To punctuate the story, Jesus asked his Jewish listeners (continuing the paraphrase of Luke 10:25-37):

> *"Which of the three passers-by was a neighbor to the beaten man?" And they said, "The one who had mercy."*

Notice how they couldn't even bring themselves to say "the Samaritan." Their resentment ran too deep. But then Jesus said:

> *"Go do the same thing, and you'll receive eternal life."*

The Good Samaritan is not a factual story; Jesus made the whole thing up. But is *The Good Samaritan* a true story? Can a story that didn't really happen still be true?

Is it true that sometimes our religion and politics get in the way of doing what is right?

Is it true that sometimes ignoble people do the noblest things?

Is it true that our suspicions of one another across racial, ethnic, and religious lines are lies straight from the pit of hell meant to divide and conquer us?

Is it true that being a child of God can be as simple as loving people the same way God first loved you?

Yeah, I think so. *The Good Samaritan*, though fiction, is a true story. It's certainly truer than *The Wolf of Wall Street*. Some stories are truer than history. Some fiction is truer than fact.

Is the Bible fact? Yes.

Is the Bible fiction? You betcha.

It's both, and that's what makes it so amazing. Dr. Bernhard Anderson, professor emeritus at Princeton Theological Seminary, summarized this paradox beautifully:

> There is a fine line between "story" and "history." If "history" means a detached report of events, the biblical story is not history. If "story" means a tale spun out of the imagination, the biblical history is not story. We are dealing with a history-like story, or a story-like history, and there is no razor sharp enough to separate these dimensions of the biblical narrative.[9]

The Bible is fact and fiction, but it's not *just* fact and fiction. It's something else, something far more compelling. I can't wait to tell you all about it, but before I do, I've got some explaining to do about the apparent dark side of the Bible.

God-Ordained Child Sacrifice?

· Every once in a while, even the most passionate lover of Scripture encounters a passage that seems morally unforgivable. Genesis 22, with its twisted tale of God proposing a child sacrifice, has likely transformed more Bible readers into *former* Bible readers than Leviticus and Revelation, combined.

Do you remember how God promised Abraham that his descendants would become a great nation? For years following that promise, there remained one fairly significant problem with God's great plan to grow a nation from the fruit of Abraham's loins.

He and Sarah were fruitless. After visiting the couple on several occasions, God finally convinced them that his promise would soon come true, and one day, after decades of trying and failing and probably even miscarrying many times, Sarah gave birth to a healthy baby boy named Isaac. Their child of promise had finally come.

Can you imagine how careful Abraham and Sarah were with Isaac? There was a lot riding on that kid—God's whole plan to save the world and all—which is why the next part of the story is so unthinkable.

> *Some time later God tested Abraham. He said to him, "Abraham!"*
>
> *"Here I am," he replied.*
>
> *Then God said, "Take your son, your only son, whom you love—Isaac—and go to the region of Moriah. Sacrifice him there as a burnt offering on a mountain I will show you." (Genesis 22:1-2)*

This is the moment that Abraham becomes an atheist, right? What kind of loving father would continue to put his trust in a God who requires child sacrifice? But Abraham didn't hesitate: he got up early the next morning and, along with Isaac and two other guys who worked for him, he set off for Moriah. When they arrived, Abraham told the two men,

> *"Stay here with the donkey while I and the boy go over there. We will worship and then we will come back to you." (Genesis 22:5)*

What was Abraham thinking? And more importantly, what was *God* thinking? As Abraham walked Isaac up the mountain, they shared what had to be the most awkward father-son talk of all time. Young Isaac knew they were going to offer an animal sacrifice to God, but he didn't see any animals around, so he asked his dad what was going on.

> Abraham answered, "God himself will provide the lamb for the burnt offering, my son." …
>
> When they reached the place God had told him about, Abraham built an altar there and arranged the wood on it. He bound his son Isaac and laid him on the altar, on top of the wood. Then he reached out his hand and took the knife to slay his son. (Genesis 22:8-10)

That escalated quickly. This is shaping up to be one of the most horrific stories you'll ever read. But hold on, there's a twist:

> But the angel of the LORD called out to him from heaven, "Abraham! Abraham!"
>
> "Here I am," he replied.
>
> "Do not lay a hand on the boy," he said. "Do not do anything to him. Now I know that you fear God, because you have not withheld from me your son, your only son." (Genesis 22:11-12)

Phew! Apparently it was never God's plan for Abraham to sacrifice Isaac at all. In the next verse, as Abraham untied his son, God provided a wild ram for the sacrifice. The ram was God's plan all along, and, if you read closely, it looks like Abraham might have known the whole time. Remember how Abraham said that both he *and* Isaac would <u>return after worshiping God</u>? And how, in response to Isaac's question about the animal for the sacrifice, Abraham said the Lord *will provide*? If Abraham believed that Isaac was going to be the sacrifice, he probably would have said, "The Lord *has already provided* it."

> ## *But let's not miss the Bible's bigger picture here: all of Scripture revolves around Jesus.*

For some people, that's still not enough because, even if he never intended for Abraham to go through with it, what kind of God would even suggest such a thing? But let's not miss the Bible's bigger picture here: all of Scripture revolves around Jesus. So when you read parts of the Bible that shock you or leave you with more questions than answers, ask yourself what that section of scripture might have to do with the life, death, and resurrection of Jesus.

So, what does this bizarre story have to do with the raucous rabbi who wasn't even born until two millennia *after* the events of Genesis 22? *Everything.* Just as so much of the Old Testament makes sense only in light of Jesus's life, death, and resurrection, the true meaning of Abraham and Isaac's dramatic journey up the mountain was exposed two thousand years later, on a hill outside Jerusalem, where Jesus was nailed to the cross.

One huge clue to the connection between Genesis 22 and the cross of Jesus is found in Abraham's own words. Most readers miss this: as the father and son walked up the mountain together, Isaac asked Abraham about the animal for the sacrifice. And how did Abraham respond?

> *"God himself will provide the lamb."* (Genesis 22:8)

But after the angel stayed Abraham's hand, what animal did God provide for the sacrifice? It was a ram, not a lamb. So why did Abraham say the offering would be a *lamb* from God?

When you piece everything together—God's outrageous command and Abraham's inexplicable compliance, along with his confidence that Isaac would be coming back down that mountain with him and his insistence that the Lord would provide a lamb even though God provided a ram—the whole story feels so cryptic and unsatisfying.

That is because Genesis 22 is just one small piece of a much larger puzzle. Of course it's disturbing to read about God telling a father to kill his own son, but this story is foreshadowing something far more consequential. More than a thousand years after the time of Abraham and Isaac, the Hebrew prophet Isaiah spoke of a man sent by God who would suffer as a sacrifice on our behalf.

> *Surely he took up our pain*
> *and bore our suffering,*
> *yet we considered him punished by God....*
> *But he was pierced for our transgressions,*
> *he was crushed for our iniquities;*
> *the punishment that brought us peace was on him,*
> *and by his wounds we are healed....*
>
> *He was led like a lamb to the slaughter,*

> *and as a sheep before its shearers is silent,*
> *so he did not open his mouth. (Isaiah 53:4-5, 7,*
> *emphasis added)*

Over six centuries after Isaiah envisioned the *lamb of God,* another prophet named John the Baptist echoed Isaiah's ancient vision when introducing Jesus to a crowd of Abraham's descendants:

> *The next day John saw Jesus coming toward him and said,*
> *"Look, the Lamb of God, who takes away the sin of the*
> *world!" (John 1:29, emphasis added)*

And a few decades later, in the aftermath of Jesus's death on the cross, the first Christians fully began to put all the pieces together:

> *For Christ, our Passover lamb, has been sacrificed.*
> *(1 Corinthians 5:7, emphasis added)*

> *For you know that it was not with perishable things such as*
> *silver or gold that you were redeemed from the empty way*
> *of life handed down to you from your ancestors, but with*
> *the precious blood of Christ, a lamb without blemish or*
> *defect. (1 Peter 1:18-19, emphasis added)*

> *Then the angel showed me the river of the water of life, as*
> *clear as crystal, flowing from the throne of God and of the*
> *Lamb. (Revelation 22:1, emphasis added)*

These are just a few examples of the dozens of passages throughout the Bible that refer to Jesus as a sacrificial lamb. Somehow, while climbing that mountain with his only son, Abraham knew that

God would provide. Consider the length of time separating the plot points along this beautiful storyline:

c. 2000 BC: *God will provide the lamb…* —Abraham
c. 650 BC: *The coming Messiah will be like a lamb…* —Isaiah
c. AD 30: *Jesus is the Lamb of God…* —John the Baptist
c. AD 50: *Our lamb has been sacrificed…* —Paul
c. AD 90: *…the throne of God and of the Lamb…* —John

For many skeptics, learning to trust the Bible as a singularly epic, true story can take years of study and life experience. Once you learn to read all sixty-six books of the Bible as one true story, however, you'll see that even the darkest parts of scripture are there for a reason: to foreshadow the Light of the world.

Many years later, the same God who told Abraham, "Now I know that you fear God, because you have not withheld from me your son, your only son," did not withhold his only Son either. Why? Love.

> *For God so loved the world that he gave his one and only Son, that whoever believes in him shall not perish but have eternal life. (John 3:16)*

Learning to Trust the Bible Again

When you hold a Bible in your hand, you hold the vast wisdom and witness of sixty-six distinct, ancient texts written by at least forty different authors who employed at least nine literary genres while writing in three languages on three continents over a span of more than fourteen hundred years.

That alone would be enough to make the Bible unique, but dig a little deeper, and you'll uncover more remarkable reasons to believe that the Bible stands apart from all other sacred texts. Its authors included murderers, priests, kings, and a guy who once baked a loaf of bread over flaming human feces (Ezekiel 4:12). Thirteen books were written by or attributed to the self-described "Chief of Sinners" (1 Timothy 1:15 KJV) and another three have been attributed to the man Jesus once called "Satan."[10]

Don't be confused by the titles of Bible books: *Psalms* is a book of songs, but *Song of Songs* is basically the Jewish *Kama Sutra*. A series of stories with the most boring name—*Judges*—might be the Bible's most entertaining book, while the Most Intriguing Book Title award goes to the apocryphal book called *Bel and the Dragon*, which sadly is boring and has no dragon.[11] You never know what you're going to get from Bible books by looking at their titles—even the book called *Numbers* includes the hilarious tale of a talking donkey (Numbers 22:21-39).

Jesus didn't write any Bible books himself, but all sixty-six books testify to the same God and his plan to save the world through the life, death, and resurrection of this mysterious, first-century rabbi from Nazareth. By many accounts, all twenty-seven New Testament books were written within a lifetime (approximately 60 years) following Jesus's death. We have around 5,800 ancient[12] Greek manuscripts of New Testament books, which equal over 2.6 million pages. Add to this the tens of thousands of New Testament manuscripts we have in Syriac, Coptic, Armenian, and Latin, as well as the remarkable *Dead Sea Scrolls* that proved the historical integrity of virtually the entire Old Testament,[13] and it becomes clear that the Bible is in a league all its own.

For the sake of comparison, the oldest copy of Plato's writings dates to about 1,400 years after Plato's life. Homer wrote his classic *The Iliad* 2,800 years ago, but the oldest fragment in existence was written 1,100 years later, and the oldest complete manuscript dates to the tenth century AD. The writings of Plato and Homer are widely respected, and you would be hard-pressed to find reputable university professors who question their authenticity.

Ardent skeptics might say, "Who cares how many fragments there are when we don't have the original copies?" It's a fair question, and you have no idea how many times I've wished the Vatican would announce that they've been hiding the originals in the papal basement all this time. Even without the original scrolls, however, the surviving manuscripts present an extraordinarily strong case for the Bible's accuracy.

Let's think about the "telephone" game again, but in reverse this time. Imagine 25,000 people who speak five different languages were told to memorize the same story in their own language. Imagine that those people all passed down the story to their children, and their children, and their children. If the great-great grandkids of the original 25,000 people all write the story down, each in their own language, and we somehow brought all 25,000 stories together, how much agreement would you expect to find among their accounts?

Seventy-five percent? Fifty? Twenty? How would you react if, despite the challenges posed by time, language, and the faulty human memory, over ninety-eight percent of the details in their written narratives perfectly aligned?

The most historically compelling fact about the almost 25,000 surviving ancient New Testament manuscripts is that they agree with one another over ninety-eight percent of the time.[14,15] Even when the manuscripts disagree, their points of departure are inconsequential, as atheist New Testament scholar Dr. Bart Ehrman acknowledged when he wrote, "Most of the changes found in our early Christian manuscripts have nothing to do with theology or ideology."[16]

Regardless of your religious persuasion, there's no denying that the Bible is unprecedented and unrivaled; the world has never seen a collection of ancient texts as old, well-preserved, and inspirational as this. Its power can cut both ways, however. The same Bible that became the banner for the abolitionists' anti-slavery struggle also served slaveowners as a means of justifying slavery and a tool for suppressing revolts. The same Bible that labeled peacemakers *blessed* (Matthew 5:9) has been wielded as a weapon to provoke countless wars. What becomes of the Bible's power depends entirely on the motives of those who use it, and therein lies the problem.

Part of the Bible's two thousand-year history involves well-intentioned Christians getting major parts of it wrong for generations at a time, until a courageous new generation cuts through the layers of legends and lies to return to the truth of the original source material. But whether or not the Christians in your life are actually *getting the Bible right* has no bearing on the objective Truth of Scripture. The Bible is either a true story or it's not, regardless of how the people who claim it behave.

A major turning point for me, and for many other former Christians who found their way back to Jesus, was learning *how to think* about the Bible for myself, instead of letting religious leaders tell me *what to think* about it. Taking a closer look at Scripture led me to a watershed moment. I realized that imperfect people have been twisting, tainting, and tearing apart the Bible for centuries, and yet the words on its pages continue to inspire and transform hundreds of thousands, if not millions, more lives across the world every year. When I finally understood the intense scrutiny and gross mishandling this book has endured and overcome, I began to respect the Scriptures more than ever before. I found myself falling in love with the Bible again.

CHAPTER THREE

ARE THE GOSPELS
RELIABLE?

The question I asked all those Houstonians—"Is the Bible fact or fiction?"—doesn't matter much when it comes to the Bible's reliability. "Fact versus Fiction" is of little consequence; what really matters is truth. *Is the Bible true?*

If you're new to the Bible, I hope you don't find this question overwhelming. It's not up to you to investigate whether or not all sixty-six books of the Bible are true. All you really have to determine is the legitimacy of Jesus. The integrity of the whole Bible rests on the legitimacy of Jesus, and the legitimacy of Jesus depends on the historicity of one event: his resurrection.

If the resurrection of Jesus didn't really happen, the Christian Bible is feckless. This assertion is as ancient as Christianity itself, as the apostle Paul wrote around AD 50:

> *But if it is preached that Christ has been raised from the*
> *dead, how can some of you say that there is no resurrection*
> *of the dead? If there is no resurrection of the dead, then*
> *not even Christ has been raised. And if Christ has not been*
> *raised, our preaching is useless and so is your faith. (1*
> *Corinthians 15:12-14)*

Before you decide what to believe about the Bible, decide what you believe about Jesus and his resurrection.

Before you decide what to believe about the Bible, decide what you believe about Jesus and his resurrection. If you decide Jesus was just another myth and his tomb was never empty, then you shouldn't continue pretending to be a Christian. If Jesus was just an inspiring teacher with overly ambitious followers who, even after his tragic (and permanent) death, refused to let his movement die, then the Bible is based on a lie and evangelical atheists like Richard Dawkins can claim victory. If these are your honest conclusions, you aren't alone; many others have explored the core Christian claims about Jesus and have subsequently rejected him.

A couple of years ago I interviewed my Religious Studies professor from Centenary College, Dr. David Otto, for an episode of the *Maybe God Podcast*. This is what he said about Jesus:

> "All the doctrine you learn and grow up with in the church…if you just look at it, it's absurd.…A Jewish

peasant, over 2,000 years ago, pissed off some Romans, was crucified, and rose from the dead three days later, continued teaching, and eventually ascended into heaven. Well, that doesn't happen very often, and it's rather absurd to make that claim, unless you have something that you can rely upon to back it up."[1]

Do Christians have anything to rely upon to back up our claims about Jesus? We have the four Gospels, but who cares? Fewer than half of all Americans can even name them.[2] Why should anyone believe these four books are remotely reliable?

New Testament scholars universally agree that, of the four biblical accounts, Mark was written first, probably around AD 60. A skeptic may sneer at the thirty-year gap between Jesus's death and alleged resurrection and Mark's Gospel, but three decades is nothing when compared to other ancient texts. When assessing the integrity of ancient literature, historians investigate the earliest known documented manuscripts, or fragments of manuscripts, that are still around today. They want to know how many manuscripts have survived and whether those manuscripts corroborate each other. Another important criterion is the number of years that passed between the actual events and the earliest writings that describe them.

When we consider the New Testament, with its 25,000 surviving, ancient manuscripts of the Gospels and other writings, nothing else comes close. Unlike the well-respected works of Greek philosophers, these surviving New Testament documents were written mere decades—not *fourteen centuries*—after the death of Jesus. If any other work of ancient literature were as well attested and long-lasting in its influence as the New Testament has been, it would be consistently lifted up as a masterpiece. In this case, however, many secular scholars make an exception. Why is it so hard to find secular academics who appreciate the historical veracity of the New Testament as much, if not more so, than that of Socrates, Plato, and Aristotle?

A Critical Question: Who Was Mark?

Once a document's historical integrity has been validated, honest historians then shift their gaze to the author's identity, context, and bias. Who was the author of the "first gospel," and why should we believe his testimony? The author of Mark's Gospel never identified himself; it would all have been much easier if Mark 1:1 said, "Hey guys, I'm Mark." But alas, we are left to piece the clues together ourselves.

Mark (a.k.a. "John Mark") first appears in the Book of Acts, which is the sequel to Luke's Gospel, after Peter had miraculously escaped prison:

> [Peter] went to the house of Mary the mother of John, also
> called Mark, where many people had gathered and were
> praying. (Acts 12:12)

Later in Acts 12, we learn that John Mark traveled with the apostle Paul and Barnabas on parts of their maiden missionary journeys (Acts 12:25). On several occasions, Paul casually mentioned John Mark in his letters (2 Timothy 4:11, Colossians 4:10, Philemon 24). Even more importantly, Simon Peter mentioned a younger man named Mark in his first New Testament letter, employing the most affectionate of terms:

> She…sends you her greetings, and so does my son Mark.
> (1 Peter 5:13)

These mentions of John Mark in the New Testament are incredibly important because they suggest that there was, in fact, a young man named Mark who had intimate access to the most influential leaders of the original church, and whom Simon Peter considered a spiritual son. The New Testament authors would not have mentioned *John Mark* so flippantly unless they could have safely assumed that most everyone in their audience was familiar with him.

When we pair these New Testament accounts with the ancient non-biblical sources who mentioned John Mark, a very strong case emerges in favor of Simon Peter as the author of the first Gospel, through the hand of his "son," who also served as his translator and scribe. Bishop Papias lived in the first century and wrote: "Mark, having become the interpreter of Peter, wrote down accurately, though not in order, whatsoever he remembered of the things said or done by Christ."[3] In the second century, a church leader named Irenaeus also pointed to Peter as the source of Mark's Gospel: "Matthew also issued a written Gospel among the Hebrews in their own dialect, while Peter and Paul were preaching at Rome, and laying the foundations of the Church. After their departure, Mark, the disciple and interpreter of Peter, did also hand down to us in writing what had been preached by Peter."[4] Other ancient sources such as Justin Martyr (c. AD 150) and Clement (c. AD 180) also identified Peter as the true voice behind Mark's Gospel.

Simon *the Rock*

With so much ancient evidence suggesting we have Peter to thank for the Gospel of Mark, and no historical evidence to the contrary, it's reasonable to assume Peter's authorship. But who was he, and why should anyone care that he "wrote" Mark's Gospel? Simon Peter was the leader of the twelve disciples; every time the Gospel writers list Jesus's entourage, they name Simon Peter first. Before Jesus called him to join the movement, Simon Peter and his brother Andrew worked for a fishing business that belonged to Zebedee, the father of John and James, two more of Jesus's key disciples.

His name wasn't really Simon Peter; *Peter* (Gk. *petros*) wasn't even a proper noun in Greek. *Petros* was a common Greek word meaning "rock," and it was the nickname Jesus gave to Simon. No one really appreciates Jesus's sense of humor anymore, but I love the fact that he gave his friends nicknames. Simon was "the Rock," James and John were "the Sons of Thunder," the other James was "Tiny," and Thomas was "the Twin."

We don't know the backstory behind every nickname Jesus handed out, but it would appear that "the Rock" was the perfect moniker for a guy like Simon. Among the twelve disciples, he was the oldest, the only one who was married, the only one who was brave enough to walk on water with Jesus, the first one to identify Jesus as the Son of God, and the only one who defended Jesus at his arrest (see, respectively, Matthew 17:27[5]; Matthew 8:14-15, 1 Corinthians 9:5; Matthew 14:29-30; Matthew 16:16; John 18:10, Matthew 26:51). Maybe it was Simon's toughness that led Jesus to look at him and proclaim:

> *"Blessed are you, Simon son of Jonah, for this was not*
> *revealed to you by flesh and blood, but by my Father in*
> *heaven. And I tell you that you are Peter, and on this rock*
> *I will build my church, and the gates of Hades will not*
> *overcome it." (Matthew 16:17-18)*

As usual with Jesus, however, his words are layered with meaning here. Simon was a tough guy, but only to a point. Once the going got tough, Simon got…*scared*. In fact, I'm 99 percent sure that when Jesus nicknamed Simon *The Rock*, it was tongue-in-cheek. It's like when you meet a really massive guy whose friends call him Tiny, you know? Simon tried to be a *rock* sometimes, but a rock is steady. A rock is consistent. A rock is *boring*, even.

Simon was none of those things. There was nothing steady, consistent, or boring about him. He was impulsive and unpredictable. Think about the day Jesus called him to be his disciple. Simon had a wife and mother in-law to feed. He most likely had kids, too. He certainly had bills to pay. But one day some cool guy said, "Follow me," and how did Simon respond? *Can I sleep on it? Think about it? Talk to my wife about it?*

Nope. Not Simon. He said, *"Does anybody need this boat? Cuz I'm a disciple now."*[6]

One night, when the disciples were sailing across the Sea of Galilee, Jesus decided to scare the bejeezus out of them by walking on water next to the boat. The disciples thought he was a ghost and started crying out to God. Jesus replied, "Guys, I'm right here." Simon Peter shot back, "If it's really you, let me walk on the water, too."

"Come on," Jesus said. So, with testosterone and hubris coursing through his veins, Simon disembarked and stood atop the surface of the sea. I imagine he and the other disciples made the typical moan-grunt noise that guys make when we can't believe what's happening right in front of us. Then Simon began to walk toward Jesus, but "when he saw the wind, he was afraid and, beginning to sink, cried out, 'Lord, save me!'" (Matthew 14:30).

Can you see why it might have been a running joke for someone like Simon to be called *The Rock*? He talked a big game, but he was really just a scared little kid on the inside. Hours before being arrested and put on trial, Jesus told his disciples, "You're all going to desert me tonight." Peter said, "Not me, Jesus. I will *never* leave you." But Jesus wasn't having it:

> Jesus answered, "I tell you, Peter, before the rooster crows
> today, you will deny three times that you know me."
> (Luke 22:34)

The Disciples *and Peter*

Just a few hours later, Jewish authorities, flanked by armed bodyguards, ambushed and detained Jesus in the Garden of Gethsemane. Peter followed the religious mob to the house where, in the cover of night, the high priest and other Sanhedrin members interrogated Jesus. It was a cold night, and Peter stood near a fire to keep warm. Three others who were there accused Peter of being a follower of the accused heretic. Three different times, bystanders said to Peter, "Weren't you with him?" The first time, Peter said, "I don't know him." Following the second accusation, he said, "I wasn't with him." And then:

> Peter replied, "Man, I don't know what you're talking
> about!" Just as he was speaking, the rooster crowed. The
> Lord turned and looked straight at Peter. Then Peter
> remembered the word the Lord had spoken to him: "Before
> the rooster crows today, you will disown me three times."
> And he went outside and wept bitterly. (Luke 22:60-62)

Can you imagine the disappointment in Jesus's eyes when he looked at his lead disciple? After all that bluster and swagger, when it mattered most, Peter failed miserably. The next morning, after Jesus was sentenced to die by crucifixion, Peter didn't even have the guts to show up. Not only was he a coward, it appears he was a quitter, too. At some point between the Last Supper on Thursday night and the resurrection on Sunday morning, Peter resigned his post. When the women went to the tomb and found it empty, the angel said to them, "Go, tell his disciples *and Peter*" (Mark 16:7, emphasis added).

So how did Peter, who was ashamed to the point of tears and resignation, later become St. Peter, the leader of the first church? There are a couple of clues in the Bible that shed some light: in the days following the resurrection of Jesus, in Luke 24, two believers went to the disciples and said, "You guys are never gonna believe this, but we just saw Jesus!" And the disciples responded: "We know Christ really has risen, and he has appeared to Simon!"

Another clue that helps us piece together a timeline of Peter's path to restoration is found in Paul's first letter to the Corinthian churches, in which he made a passing mention of Peter's private *come-to-Jesus meeting*:

> *Christ died for our sins,…was buried,…was raised on the*
> *third day,…and…he appeared to [Peter],[7] and then to the*
> *[other disciples]. (1 Corinthians 15:3-5, emphasis added)*

Peter, Do You Love Me?

Why do you think Jesus had a secret meeting with Peter first, before appearing to the other disciples? It looks like he wanted to get his *Rock* back. And it worked because, soon after their little talk, Peter started hanging out with the disciples again. In John 21, they went fishing all night long, but they didn't catch much. They decided to call it a day at about six in the morning, so they headed for the shore. When they were about a hundred yards out, they noticed a man, hanging out on the beach, building a fire. Weird. *Who builds a fire on the beach at six in the morning?*

The man stood up and yelled something like, "Hey boys, if you're having trouble finding the fish, try throwing out the nets on the other side of the boat…that works every time!"

Immediately, the disciples realized what was going on. It wasn't just some weirdo building a fire on the shoreline; it was *Jesus*. Then this happened: "When Simon Peter heard that it was [Jesus], he put on some clothes, for he was naked, and jumped into the sea" (John 21:7 NRSV).

That has to be the funniest line in Scripture. After fishing naked, Peter got so excited when he saw Jesus on the shore that he put his clothes back on *and then jumped into the water*. The Rock was officially *back*!

As Peter swam ashore, he saw and smelled the fire Jesus was building. It wasn't an ordinary fire; John's Gospel is very clear that it was a *charcoal fire* (Gk. *anthrakia*). Only two charcoal fires are mentioned in the entire Bible: the first was the one where Peter warmed himself as he denied knowing Jesus three times.

Why did Jesus start a charcoal fire? To re-create a scene that Peter would have preferred to forget. After they finished breakfast, Jesus asked a series of questions that, given the circumstances, must have felt to Peter like a punch in the gut:

Jesus: "Do you love me?"
Peter: "You know that I love you."
Jesus: "Do you love me?"
Peter: "You know that I love you."
Jesus: "Do you love me?"

Something about this third question really bothered Peter. John 21:17 (NRSV) says Peter "felt hurt" by his master's phrasing. Still, Peter pulled himself together and responded, "You know everything; you know that I love you." And Jesus said, "Feed my sheep" (John 21:17 NRSV).

You've probably heard how there are several words for "love" in Greek, the language in which the New Testament was written:

Philia is the most basic form of love. It's "love you, bro" love.

Storge is the love shared within a family. It's "I love my mommy" love.

Eros is intimate and sexual. It's "Let's get it on" love.

Then there is *agape*, which is the highest form of love. *Agape* is the perfect love of God. This is really important to know because, in this exchange with Peter, Jesus uses two different words for love, but the distinction Jesus made is completely lost in the English language.

The first time Jesus asked Peter, "Do you love me?" he said *Peter, me agapas?* In other words, *Peter, do you love me like I love you?* But Peter responded, *Phileo su,* or *I love you, but not that much.* So Jesus asked him the same question: *Peter, me agapas?* But again, Peter said, *Phileo su.*

Why would Peter answer Jesus this way? In a word, shame. The memory of what he'd done, compounded by the familiar aroma of burning charcoal, overcame him. For Peter, that wound was still so fresh that he could not bring himself to tell Jesus, "I love you as much as you love me." What happened next is one of the most beautiful moments in all of Scripture, and it is entirely lost in the English language.

In English, it appears that Jesus asked Peter the same question— *Do you love me?*—a third time, but that's not really what happened. Instead, with his third question, Jesus acquiesced to Peter's present state of mind and asked, *Peter, me phileas?*

If you've heard this story before, perhaps you've wondered why Peter felt hurt after Jesus asked the same question three times. Was Peter offended by Jesus's repetition? No, it's so much deeper than that. Peter felt hurt because he forced Jesus to come down to his level.

In response to Jesus's third question, Peter said once more, *Phileo su,* as if to say, "Yes, it's true. I love you, Jesus, but not the way you love me. Not the way you deserve to be loved. I love you, but my love is basic." How did Jesus respond to Peter's admissions of imperfect love? He looked his fallen disciple in the eyes and said, "Feed my sheep."

Peter's love wasn't perfect, but that day, it was enough for Jesus. From that day on, Peter led the Jesus movement with steady,

> *Peter's love wasn't perfect, but that day,*
> *it was enough for Jesus.*

consistent courage. After spending just a few short years close to Jesus, Peter actually became the *Rock* that Jesus saw in him all along. If Mark, as all available evidence suggests, served as Peter's scribe and recorded his firsthand accounts of the time he spent with Jesus, the Gospel of Mark is certainly a reliable source of truth.

If Mark Was True, Why Did They Write Three More?

New Testament scholars generally agree that Matthew and Luke were written five to ten years after Mark. They are both slightly longer than Mark, and they both copied large sections of Mark while also supplementing additional details, stories, and teachings that were important to them. Over half (56 percent) of Matthew and just under half (42 percent) of Luke match Mark, almost verbatim. Strangely enough, when you examine the sections of Matthew and Luke that weren't borrowed from Mark, there is a significant amount of material they share in common. Almost one-quarter of Matthew matches Luke, word for word. We're left to assume that they both had in their possession a prior source that was *not* Mark.

Despite their penchant for plagiarism, Matthew and Mark did write some of their own material as well. One-fifth of Matthew appears to be original to Matthew, while one-third of Luke is exclusive to Luke. If you really want to know what agendas compelled Matthew and Luke to write their own biographies of Jesus, the unique contributions of each author would be the best passages to scrutinize.

Matthew's particular agenda is settled science among Bible scholars. Whereas Mark reads like an action-packed, no-frills play-by-play, Matthew referenced or directly quoted the Hebrew Bible ninety-six times, such as this addendum that he tacked on to the end of a passage in which Jesus healed a long line of sick people:

> *This was to fulfill what was spoken through the prophet Isaiah:*
>
> *"He took up our infirmities*
> *and bore our diseases." (Matthew 8:17)*

None of the other Gospel writers quoted the Hebrew Bible half as much as Matthew does. Unlike the Gospel of Mark, Matthew begins with a (very Jewish) family tree, advertising the genealogical thread that ran from Abraham, through King David, and straight to Jesus (Matthew 1:1-17). Matthew is the only Gospel that puts the spotlight on Joseph, rather than Mary, to demonstrate Joseph's Jewish identity as well as his exceptional faith in God (Matthew 1:18–2:23). Matthew also includes certain parables of Jesus that spoke primarily to his Hebrew audience.[8]

The only logical reason why Matthew went out of his way to make connections between the Hebrew Bible and Jesus is because his target audience was Jewish. As a devout Jew himself, Matthew wanted other Jews to know that Jesus was more than just a rabbi; he was the Messiah, foretold by Scripture. It appears that, although Matthew trusted the reliability of Mark enough to copy most of it verbatim, he was also inspired by the Spirit of God to write a more pointed Gospel for his Jewish community.

Luke's agenda appears to have been unique as well. As the only known Gentile author of a Bible book, Luke sought to build off of Mark's foundation by highlighting the love that Jesus had for Gentiles. The first-century world was considerably more tribal than our world is today; no one outside of the Jewish community would have anticipated a Jewish Messiah with good intentions for the world beyond Judaism. Luke wrote with a Gentile audience in mind, clearly seeking to demonstrate the global nature of the gospel.

Luke was also a *Social Justice Warrior*. Of the four Gospels, only Luke includes Mary's Song, in which the mother of Jesus proclaimed that her son's kingdom would bring economic justice to the world:

> *He has brought down rulers from their thrones*
> *but has lifted up the humble.*
> *He has filled the hungry with good things*
> *but has sent the rich away empty. (Luke 1:52-53)*

Luke is also the only Gospel to give us *The Good Samaritan* story, which features two Jewish villains and a non-Jewish hero. Jesus in the Gospel of Luke is also much more critical of the Pharisees and other Jewish leaders than he is in the other three Gospels. In Jesus's fascinating *Parable of the Great Banquet*, which is also found in Matthew's Gospel, Luke emphasizes the party host's insistence that his house be full of people—no matter where they come from:

> *"The servant came back and reported [the absence of his*
> *invited guests] to his master.... [He] became angry and*

> *ordered his servant, 'Go out quickly into the streets and*
> *alleys of the town and bring in the poor, the crippled, the*
> *blind and the lame.'*
>
> *"'Sir,' the servant said, 'what you ordered has been done,*
> *but there is still room.'*
>
> *"Then the master told his servant, 'Go out to the roads*
> *and country lanes and compel them to come in, so that my*
> *house will be full.'" (Luke 14:21-23)*

To be clear, "*Go out to the roads and country lanes*" was a mandate from Jesus to extend God's invitation to those outside of Israel. When Luke, who also wrote the New Testament book called the *Acts of the Apostles*, sat down to write his Gospel, he obviously had in mind the salvation of the Gentiles.

The Gospel of John stands apart from the other three in tone and style, but this should come as no surprise. Many believe that John, who was a close personal friend of Jesus and the adopted son of Mary (John 19:25-27), wrote his Gospel at least two decades later than the others. By the time he put pen to parchment, every detail of Mark, Matthew, and Luke was well-known among all the Christians, so instead of rehashing familiar stories, John approached the task of Gospel-writing from a more spiritual perspective. For example, instead of starting the story in the beginning of Jesus's life on earth, John began with the beginning of time itself:

> *In the beginning was the Word, and the Word was with*
> *God, and the Word was God....*
>
> *The Word became flesh and made his dwelling among us.*

We have seen his glory, the glory of the one and only
Son, who came from the Father, full of grace and truth.
(John 1:1, 14)

John told the gospel story with soul. In his old age, John told the stories of Jesus from heaven's perspective. Things appear to occur out of order, Jesus's teachings are often so deep that no one can understand him (John 16:16-18), and we get a more intimate look at Jesus's spiritual life, such as the beautiful, lengthy prayers he offered on his disciples' behalf (John 17).

Once I tried to explain all of this to my kids, and my twelve year-old daughter said, "It's kinda like how Lin-Manuel Miranda told the story of Alexander Hamilton, right?" At first I laughed it off. "No sweetheart, the Gospel of John is not like a Broadway musical." But the more I thought about her point, the more sense it made to me. When John wrote his Gospel, he built off of published history (the other Gospels, Paul's letters, and so forth) and added passion, poetry, and a more transcendent perspective.

Zaira Joelle, if you're reading this, you were right. The Gospel of John is kinda like *Hamilton*.

Why Do the Four Gospels Appear to Contradict Each Other?

A very common arrow in the quiver of some Bible critics is the argument that the biblical story of Jesus is unreliable because the four Gospels don't even agree about what happened. When you read the four accounts of the Easter story, for example, they appear to disagree with one another at several points throughout the narrative:

- How many women went to visit the tomb of Jesus on Easter morning? Matthew says two, Mark says three, Luke mentions at least four, and John names only one.

- How many angels were waiting at the tomb when the women arrived? Matthew and Mark say there was only one angel. Luke said there were two angels. John didn't mention a single angel, which seems like a glaring omission.

- Were there guards at Jesus's tomb, and was there an earthquake on the first Easter morning? Matthew says yes to both, but none of the others mention an earthquake or any guards at the tomb.

What is with all these discrepancies? If you're skeptical about Christianity and you come across this information, you might feel like throwing up your hands and walking away. Is it really asking too much of Matthew, Mark, Luke, and John that they get their story straight about, you know, *the most important event in the history of the world*?

At first blush, this would appear to discredit the Resurrection story, but let's look at this problem another way. Imagine that you have four adolescent children living at home (scary, I know) and, after a night out on the town with your spouse, you return to find the house in total disarray. *Something bad has happened here*, you think to yourself, so you call each kid, one at a time, into your room to hear their version of what happened.

Now imagine if they all told you exactly the same story, word for word, with no discrepancies or differing details. Imagine that your eighteen-year-old daughter gave you the very same excuse that your thirteen-year-old son gave, even though you know them to have very different personalities. Being the savvy parent that you are, you're going to be extremely suspicious of the story they concocted and rehearsed to perfection.

You can apply the same line of reasoning to the four Gospel accounts of the first Easter. Imagine if, instead of four distinct accounts where some of the details differ, we had four Resurrection stories that were all exactly the same. Imagine if Matthew, Mark, Luke, and John, who all wrote their Gospels in different times and places, and for different audiences, recorded the Easter miracle in lockstep with one another. Would that add credibility to their case, or would that raise even more questions? It would reek of collusion!

During my journey from anti-Christian cynicism toward abiding faith in the God of Scripture, I came to the realization that the minor discrepancies found in the Gospels actually lend *more* credibility to their story, instead of detracting from it. This is especially true when you consider that all four Gospels absolutely agree on the only fact that really mattered on the first Easter morning: the tomb was empty.

CHAPTER FOUR

What Is the Bible About?

Seeing Jesus for who he is can be a terrifying prospect for people who take pride in their own intellect. I'm writing from experience here; surrendering to Jesus was the most humiliating thing I've ever done. But Truth is Truth, and when I saw it, I could no longer deny it. Those who examine the facts around Jesus's life and determine that he is for real then must come to terms with the trustworthiness of the book that attests to him. If the tomb is really empty, and Jesus is truly God, then it's more than reasonable to trust the Bible. The *whole* Bible.

Like many people, I used to struggle to accept parts of the Old Testament, but Jesus loved the Old Testament and quoted it often.[1] He never condemned, condescended, or contradicted it like I used to. If anything, he enhanced it. In his longest and most famous sermon, Jesus dealt extensively with the Old Testament, and he insisted that trusting the Law of Moses and the Hebrew prophets is not optional for believers. As far as Jesus is concerned, the Hebrew Bible is the everlasting Word of God:

> *"Do not think that I have come to abolish the Law or the Prophets; I have not come to abolish them but to fulfill them. For truly I tell you, until heaven and earth disappear, not the smallest letter, not the least stroke of a pen, will by any means disappear from the Law until everything is accomplished." (Matthew 5:17-18)*

After more than a decade of dismissing and disrespecting the Old Testament, my newfound love for Jesus led me to take another look at his Word, and when I read it again through the lens of his love, I was blown away. The Old Testament is the story of a desperate, merciless world full of violence, war, slavery, and oppression; its authors described their reality as honestly as they could. Their world was a dark place, so instead of clutching our pearls when we find darkness in the Bible, maybe we should wonder if the Old Testament perfectly depicts the world as they knew it—a broken world in need of nothing less than Jesus.

That's how Jesus looked at Scripture. Once I learned to trust him, I also learned to trust the Bible. Whereas before I opened the *Good Book* expecting to find something suspicious, now I open it knowing I'll find something true.

It's a Love Story

I had my first drink of beer at a Cincinnati Reds game when I was six years old. It was the summer of 1985, and my great-aunt Corinne, then in her 60s, convinced my parents to let her take me on a rust-belt road trip. First, we took the Amtrak from Texas to West Virginia, where her adult son, my second cousin Bruce, took me hiking up the Appalachians. To celebrate my first time seeing mountains, he handed me a kid-sized wad of *Red Man* chewing tobacco, and I pretended to know what to do with it. Did I mention I was six?

The next night, great-aunt Corinne took second cousin Bruce and me to watch Pete Rose's Cincinnati Reds host the Pittsburgh Pirates. Rose was my favorite player, and that was the year he broke Ty Cobb's record to become baseball's all-time hits leader. According to federal investigators, it was also the year that Rose (who somehow played for *and* head-coached the Reds) decided it might be fun to place illegal bets on Reds' games.

I decided to take a little gamble of my own that night. Around the sixth inning, great-aunt Corinne ordered two pints of something called *Old Milwaukee*. When the vendor handed her the plastic souvenir cups, I asked her what was in them. "It's beer," she said. In shock, I froze. A stiff Ohio wind would've knocked me over like a cardboard cutout. I was a Bible Belt kid; I had never even *seen* beer before, much less watch a trusted adult drink some. "Can I try it?" I asked. She hesitated until second cousin Bruce chimed in, "Let the boy have a swig; he handled that *Red Man* like a champ!" I grinned with pride.

Great-aunt Corinne handed me the cup, and I took a sip. It was disgusting. I wanted more chewing tobacco just to get the beer taste out of my mouth. Thanks to great-aunt Corinne and second cousin Bruce, I grew up thinking all beer tasted like *Old Milwaukee*, a belief that served me well through my adolescence in the deep South. It's much easier to be a Bible-thumper when you're pretty sure that beer's active ingredient is battery acid.

In high school, I tried really hard to be a good Christian who was committed to sobriety, sexual purity, and spending Saturday nights at home, ironing my Sunday clothes. I was the boy every dad hoped his daughter would date; that's the reason so few girls ever wanted to date me.

Well, it was *among* the reasons.

When I was twenty and in college, I learned a few things about my childhood religion, like how Jesus drank real wine and how there's an entire book in the Bible dedicated to the celebration of sensual love and passion. Sardonic professors of philosophy and religion informed lecture halls packed with impressionable young minds that the Bible was no different from every other ancient holy book: it was written by men who employed archaic conceptions of god to help people make sense of their existence and to ease their fears of mortality with promises of paradise in the afterlife. The Bible, they said, is a highly edited, poorly translated collection of ancient myths, and its historical plausibility is on par with the latest *Star Wars* film.

Upon learning that the book I had given my entire life to was basic fiction, my initial reaction, naturally, was "Wait...*why am I still a virgin?*" I no longer believed in the God of the Bible, but I was also furious with him for keeping me "pure" all those years for no good reason. So, after spending my teens telling everybody why they should believe in the Bible, I spent much of my twenties telling people why they shouldn't.

It's patriarchal and violent.
It contradicts itself.
It's poorly translated and deeply flawed.

One night in my late twenties, I was invited to something called *Theology on Tap*, which was advertised as a public forum for believers and skeptics to engage in meaningful conversation but actually was just an excuse for young Christians to get drunk together. The same shock that froze me twenty years earlier at Riverfront Stadium came over me again; I had never seen Christians drinking alcohol in the same room together. Somebody handed me something called a *Boulevard Wheat* from the local microbrewery, and let me tell you—it was nothing like the *Old Milwaukee* my great-aunt Corinne gave me. It was sublime.

As I sat at the bar pondering what other wonders I'd missed out on thanks to this God I no longer believed in, the event emcee introduced two men to the crowd. One fellow appeared to be in his fifties and wore glasses, penny-loafers, and a sweater-vest. He could have been forty, but the sweater-vest added at least ten years. He was cleanly shaven, and his thinning hair was parted neatly down one side.

The other guy was basically the Christian version of Ryan Gosling: young and handsome with messy blonde hair, a five o'clock shadow, and biceps as big as my thighs. Standing next to each other, they looked like the old "Mac vs. PC" commercials, where the cool kid makes fun of dorks who still use *Windows*, so when the emcee announced that they would be debating theology, I actually felt sorry for Dr. Sweater-Vest. Nothing he could possibly say that night would be enough to overcome the obvious appeal of Mr. Biceps.

The debate began with the emcee asking both presenters to describe, in the simplest, most succinct way possible, why they iden-tified as Christians instead of something else. Mr. Biceps went first, and after starting with a joke that really wasn't funny but everybody laughed because we all wanted him to like us, he meandered through an endless series of dry, academic treatises. Claiming to make an air-tight case for the Christian faith, he used words like antinomianism, penal substitution, and hypostatic union. Thirty minutes later, he was still going strong, but the room was lost. Mr. Biceps had done the impossible; he made a bar full of young people sick of looking at him.

I was about to head home when the emcee mercifully called time-of-death on the never-ending lecture and asked Dr. Sweater-Vest the same question, "Why are you a Christian, instead of something else?" Looking up at the ceiling, he fidgeted with his shirt collar and took a deep breath; quietly, he told us a story.

> *There once was a boy who had everything but felt he had nothing.*
> *He deeply resented his father for never giving him what he deserved.*
> *So one day the boy looked his dad in the eye and said,*
> *"You're dead to me, jackass!" and he left his father's house.*

The room fell silent. No one could believe Dr. Sweater-Vest said *jackass* at *Theology on Tap*. Then, with the entire bar in the palm of his hand, he kept going:

> *At last, the boy was free from his father; that was all he ever wanted.*
> *But to his dismay, the deep, empty feeling remained.*
> *One dreadful day it hit him: "Oh no. Maybe I'm the problem.*
> *Dad gave me everything and all he asked of me was love."*
> *Bankrupt and alone, the boy went home, trembling with fear.*
> *As he walked slowly, shamefully up the path toward the house,*
> *he saw his father running toward him with a crazed look in his eyes.*
> *"He's finally going to give me what I deserve," the boy thought.*

And he braced himself for a beating.
But all the boy got was a kiss, new clothes, and a party.

Dr. Sweater-Vest handed the microphone back to the emcee. In forty seconds, he did what Mr. Biceps failed to do in forty minutes; he explained the whole Bible with one simple story. Obviously, it wasn't his original material—Jesus told the *Prodigal* story (without saying *jackass*) two thousand years before (Luke 15:11-32)—but later that night, Dr. Sweater-Vest explained how he was actually the boy in the story. Somehow, an ancient Jewish rabbi told a story starring Dr. Sweater-Vest almost *two thousand years before sweater-vests even existed.*

Sitting in that bar, I knew I was the boy, too. My whole life, I had it all—good health, loving family, plenty of food, clean water, shelter, education, *Red Man Chew*—and for years I'd behaved like a spoiled little brat. Although I had everything, I always felt entitled to a little something more, just like Pete Rose in 1985.

Later that night, Dr. Sweater-Vest said something else I'll never forget. "Most of you were raised to read the Bible like it's a textbook for the most important class of your life," he said. "And you've been told that, at the end of the class, there will be a pass/fail test on the material in the book. If that's how you're reading the Bible, you still haven't learned to read it. It's a love story; not a textbook!"

It took a few years for me to figure out what Dr. Sweater-Vest shook loose in my heart that night, but I see it so clearly now. All my life, I thought the Bible was disappointing because my expectations of it were simply too high. Now I see that, whenever the Bible has disappointed me, it's been because my expectations were far too low.

> *Now I see that, whenever the Bible has disappointed me, it's been because my expectations were far too low.*

It's not only about long-ago people. *It's also about me.*
It's not a theological beating. *It's a father's embrace.*
It's not a textbook. *It's a love story.*

But Is This Love for Real?

Like any love story, the Bible has a past—not only the history contained in its narrative, but the book itself has a story to tell. Have you ever held a Bible and wondered, *How did this book even get here? Why has it been protected, preserved, and passed down more than any other book before or since? And in the age of science and reason, why does this book still matter at all?*

Let's take these questions from our modern context and work our way backward. Today, there is no escaping the Bible. More than two-thirds of the world's population (Jews, Christians, and Muslims) build their lives around it. No matter where you live in the United States, or what you believe about God, you are surrounded daily by countless symbolic, scriptural allusions. Presidents, judges, and other elected officials take their oaths of office while placing their hands on it. The most fundamental American values, such as the "unalienable rights endowed by the Creator," the equal worth of every human life, and representative democracy were all inspired by it.

Even Americans who have never read the *Good Book* are sure to quote it often, as the Judeo-Christian scriptures have seeped into secular parlance with universally familiar phrases such as *forbidden fruit* (Genesis 3), *eat, drink, and be merry* (Ecclesiastes 8:15), *the blind leading the blind* (Matthew 15:13-14), *a fly in the ointment* (Ecclesiastes 10:1), *go the extra mile* (Matthew 5:41), *the writing is on the wall* (Daniel 5), and *can a leopard change his spots?* (Jeremiah 13:23).

Any outside observer of our cultural milieu would expect to find a citizenry that deeply admires the Bible. Although this book permeates every parcel of American life, most of us are oblivious about its influence. Recent studies reveal our growing ambivalence toward the Bible; almost six in ten adults in the US don't read it at all or rarely read it. Two in ten are "Bible-friendly" and read the Bible consistently but may not use it as a source of insight and wisdom, while another two in ten interact with the Bible frequently, with transformation in their relationships with God and others. Only one in *twenty* American adults claim to be "Bible-centered," meaning not only do they read it frequently, but they also allow its words to transform their relationships and direct their steps.[2]

So why do so few Americans read the Bible, and why do even fewer of us *love* it? The great evangelical preacher D. L. Moody is often quoted as saying, "Out of one hundred men, one will read the Bible, and the other ninety-nine will read the Christian." Sometimes all it takes for a skeptic to object to the Christian Bible is for him or her to spend a little time with morally objectionable Christians.

Make no mistake: people have said and done some awful things with Bibles in their hands. I've witnessed outspoken believers publicly demeaning women, condemning gays, shaming skeptics, and trolling liberals on social media. We've all watched politicians manipulate the Bible and the people who love it for their own political ends. Some Christians have a way of making the greatest love story ever told seem wholly unloving.

Sometimes it's hard for Christians to understand why so many people think the Bible is problematic, but maybe we're not being very good listeners. If it's true that most everyone loves a love story, but more people every day are falling out of love with the Bible, then it stands to reason that many people no longer think the Bible is a love story. I've known plenty of folks who have trouble believing that the Bible is about true love, usually for one of three reasons:

- They grew up in a hardcore, hellfire-and-brimstone kind of church, and now they reject all things Christian.
- They are part of a group of people who've historically been marginalized by Christians.
- They grew up in a secular home, and all they know about Christianity they learned from the news media, social media, or other tertiary sources that have informed them that the Bible is antiquated, anti-women, and pro-slavery.

Some people have other reasons for believing the Bible is not about love, but these are the three I've found to be most common. Each one of these reasons can be supported by proof-texting (the art of carefully selecting an out-of-context Bible verse and using it to make your point). There really is hellfire-and-brimstone in the Bible. Some people actually are marginalized in certain parts of scripture.

If you were so inclined, you could also find a few verses to support the notion that the Bible is outdated, sexist, and pro-slavery.

But let's be honest: proof-texting is lazy and irresponsible. I should know. I used to proof-text the Bible better than anyone. But even if you don't agree with the Jewish or Christian worldviews, the Bible itself deserves a more honest analysis than proof-texting can afford. It is thousands of years old, it's sacred to almost six billion people, and it's the best-selling book in history. The least we can do is try to see it for what it really is.

Love: The One Common Thread

The sixty-six books that make up the Bible deal with many different themes. Religion, by which I mean the practice of regulating behavior and repeating rituals in order to curry favor with God, appears to be a major theme in the Bible, but when you take a discerning look at the New Testament, it's so clear that Jesus was introducing something beyond religion. God's wrath—his divine anger at human sin—plays a prominent role in both testaments, but it was no longer a concern among the first Christians because there was "no condemnation for those who are in Christ Jesus" (Romans 8:1). So God's wrath is not the primary theme in Scripture.

Other themes come and go in the Bible, but there is only one common, thematic thread woven throughout every patch of the biblical tapestry: love. Love infuses the Scriptures from cover to cover, from the fourth chapter of Genesis, when the first two humans "made love," to the twentieth chapter of Revelation, when God expressed love for his eternal city, and six hundred eighty-four other times.

> *For God so loved the world that he gave his one and only Son. (John 3:16)*

> *"Greater love has no one than this: to lay down one's life for one's friends." (John 15:13)*

> *Now faith, hope, and love abide, these three; but the greatest of these is love. (1 Corinthians 13:13 ESV)*

> *We love because he first loved us. (1 John 4:19)*

> *Whoever does not love does not know God, for God is love. (1 John 4:8 NRSV)*

Of course, not everyone agrees that God is love. Richard Dawkins, perhaps the most outspoken atheist in the world, once posited, "The God of the Old Testament is arguably the most unpleasant character in all fiction."[3] American revolutionary and philosopher Thomas Paine wrote, "It is not a God, just and good, but a devil...that the Bible describes."[4] The late author Christopher Hitchens opined, "The Bible...does contain a warrant for trafficking in humans, for ethnic cleansing, for slavery, for bride-price, and for indiscriminate massacre, but we are not bound by any of it because it was put together by crude, uncultured human mammals."[5]

Men like Dawkins, Paine, and Hitchens claim to live according to the laws of reason. They see everything through a materialistic, Darwinian lens. Everything must be proven—even love—and reasonable people must never believe in something without sufficient empirical evidence. In a letter he wrote to his ten-year-old daughter, Dawkins attempted to explain love from his rational perspective:

People sometimes say that you must believe in feelings deep inside, otherwise you'd never be confident of things like 'My wife loves me'. But this is a bad argument. There can be plenty of evidence that somebody loves you. All through the day when you are with somebody who loves you, you see and hear lots of little tidbits of evidence, and they all add up. It isn't a purely inside feeling, like the feeling that priests call revelation. There are outside things to back up the inside feeling: looks in the eye, tender notes in the voice, little f1ors and kindnesses; this is all real evidence.[6]

While I appreciate Dawkins' effort to make room for love in his scientific worldview, there are some obvious problems with his definition of love. If evidence is required to prove that you love someone, how much evidence is necessary, and how often must such evidence be produced? If you looked your wife in the eye and spoke to her with tender notes in the voice on your wedding day, but you haven't done so again since then, do you love her? You've got wedding pictures and videos that prove how you looked at her and spoke to her—real evidence! But is that love?

You may be thinking, "But people fall out of love. It might have been real love on the wedding day, but things change." Fair enough. But what if every day for twenty years, a man looks his wife in the eye and speaks tenderly to her, offering evidence of his love for her, but then he falls into a deep depression and suddenly lacks the cognitive resources to prove his love as he once did? Should we say he no longer loves her?

Or what if, as was the case in past generations, the man was sent off to war and unable to write home for months, or even years at a time? If he still thinks of her, dreams of her, and prays for her every day, but she can't see or hear him, does he love her? In the absence of real evidence, are we to believe this soldier's wife is unloved?

Or what if, for years, a man shows his wife real evidence of love—sincere glances, tender words, and flowers every Valentine's Day—but all the while, unbeknownst to her, he has a mistress across town? Despite all her evidence to the contrary, it's safe to say that she was never really loved.

Love cannot be reduced to mere data and facts. To believe in love requires faith, and therein lies the problem for many of us today. Although we claim to be committed to a secular worldview that is based on empirical evidence, we can't stop believing in love.

What Is Love?

The authors of the Bible offer no shortage of well-known extraordinary claims, but Scripture's most audacious proposition is found hidden away in a little-known letter toward the end of the New Testament:

> God is love. (1 John 4:16)

Even if you're not a believer, this is an absolutely stunning idea. The Bible doesn't just say, "God gives love," or "God wants love," or "God expects love." The outrageous Christian claim is that God IS love. Love is God's essence. Love isn't what God *does*; love is who God *is*. In every section of Scripture, the love of God shines through the world's darkness. In the Bible's second book, called Exodus, when Moses and the Hebrews were still just getting to know God, this is how God described himself:

> *"The LORD, the LORD, the compassionate and gracious*
> *God, slow to anger, abounding in love and faithfulness,*
> *maintaining love to thousands, and forgiving wickedness,*
> *rebellion and sin." (Exodus 34:6-7, emphasis added)*

In the New Testament, the oft-maligned and misunderstood apostle Paul reeled off the most famous, and most beautiful, words ever written about love:

> *If I speak in the tongues of men or of angels, but do not*
> *have love, I am only a resounding gong or a clanging*
> *cymbal. If I have the gift of prophecy and can fathom all*
> *mysteries and all knowledge, and if I have a faith that*
> *can move mountains, but do not have love, I am nothing.*
> *If I give all I possess to the poor and give over my body to*
> *hardship that I may boast, but do not have love, I gain*
> *nothing. (1 Corinthians 13:1-3)*

Maybe you've heard those verses a hundred times at weddings, so you think they're played out. Read it again, and ask yourself, "Where did a buttoned-down bachelor like Paul find the inspiration to define love so eloquently?" Isn't this the same guy who advised single Christians against getting married (1 Corinthians 7:28)? Wasn't Paul infamous for his Pharisaic allegiance to the rules? How did this virginal stickler become the world's leading expert on love?

It was Jesus. For the first half of his life, Paul was a religious fundamentalist. Following the resurrection of Jesus, as the Christian uprising began to threaten the status quo, Temple leaders in Jerusalem ordered Paul—then a young Pharisee—to stamp out the rebellion. After he oversaw the first wave of widespread, violent persecution of

Christians, during which families were dragged out of their homes and some were beaten or thrown in jail, Paul supervised the murder of Stephen, the first Christian martyr (Acts 7:54-60). And with Stephen's blood still fresh on the pavement, Paul was on his way to Damascus to terrorize more Christians, but something happened that altered the course of his life: he had a personal experience with Jesus (Acts 9:1-19).

From that day on, everything changed. Paul's old friends now hated him, while his new companions—his "brothers and sisters" in Christ—were understandably slow to trust him. He had built his entire identity—including his career, his goals, and his social connections—around being a zealous Pharisaic Jew. Believing in Jesus not only meant Paul had to start over, it also meant Paul would have to repeatedly, profusely apologize to all his new colleagues for, you know, trying to murder them all last week.

When Paul wrote his most famous lines about love in 1 Corinthians 13 that we've heard at all the weddings—"Love is patient, love is kind…"—it wasn't just the emotion of *love* that he had in mind. That actually wouldn't make sense in context of the rest of his first letter to the Corinthians. Chapter 12 is all about the body of Christ, and chapter 14 is all about worshiping Christ. So why would Paul interrupt this deep teaching with a sappy love poem in chapter 13?

I don't think he did. No—I think Paul was still writing about Jesus in 1 Corinthians 13. In fact, I think that's the only way to make sense of Paul's most famous passage. For Paul, Jesus was the perfect representation of love, so whenever you read the *Love* chapter, try replacing the word "love" with "Jesus." What you'll find is the most comprehensive description in the entire Bible of who Jesus is:

> *Jesus is patient, Jesus is kind. He does not envy, he does not*
> *boast, he is not proud. He does not dishonor others, he is*
> *not self-seeking, he is not easily angered, he keeps no record*
> *of wrongs. Jesus does not delight in evil but rejoices with*
> *the truth. He always protects, always trusts, always hopes,*
> *always perseveres. Jesus never fails. (1 Corinthians 13:4-8,*
> *adapted)*

Paul was respected before meeting Jesus. He was really going places. He was making his devout Jewish parents proud. But the day Paul encountered Jesus, he found real love, and everybody knows that when you find real love, you chase it because love is the thing that matters most. Paul turned his life upside-down, all for Jesus, who loved Paul long before Paul ever loved him back.

> *But God demonstrates his own love for us in this:* While
> we were still sinners, Christ died for us. *(Romans 5:8,*
> *emphasis added)*

Looking for Love in All the Wrong Places

After narrowly escaping the child sacrifice scare in Genesis 22, Isaac grew up to live a pretty good life alongside his wife, Rebekah, and their sons, Esau and Jacob. Although they were twins, the two brothers were nothing alike. Esau was everything a young man was supposed to be back then: big, hairy, and hungry. Jacob, on the other hand, was lazy and soft. He also had a major character flaw, as evidenced by his name, which literally meant *deceiver*. After lying multiple times to cheat Esau out of their father's blessing, Jacob ran for the hills to avoid being slaughtered by his bigger, stronger brother (Genesis 27:41-43).

Jacob landed on his feet and found a good job working for a man named Laban, but his erratic and desperate behavior continued. One day, Laban asked him to name his own salary, and Jacob said, "Your daughter's hot. I'll take her." No, seriously:

> Now Laban had two daughters; the name of the older was
> Leah, and the name of the younger was Rachel. Leah had
> weak eyes, but Rachel had a lovely figure and was beautiful.
> Jacob was in love with Rachel and said, "I'll work for you
> seven years in return for your younger daughter Rachel."
> (Genesis 29:16-18)

So this story says Rachel had a "lovely figure" and that she was "beautiful" which is nice, but even so, Jacob's actions made no sense. Seven years is a *long* time . . . and Jacob barely even knew Rachel! He sounds a lot like the guy who says "I love you" on the second date, or the girl you just met who "likes" everything you ever posted on Instagram at three o'clock in the morning.

You've known someone like Jacob before. All he really wanted was his father's approval, but it was always just beyond his reach. His dad was blind, so one time Jacob changed his voice and pretended to be Esau just to know what it felt like to be loved by his dad (Genesis 27:1-24). He'd been running from the truth all his life, and in this story he acted like a man who was running from the past. But no matter how far you run, the truth will always catch up to you. That's what happened to Jacob.

After working under Laban for seven years, Jacob could finally claim his prize—the lovely Rachel. He said to Laban, "Give me my wife. My time is completed, and I want to make love to her" (Genesis 29:21), which is a very odd thing to say to your future father in-law. If a young man ever says anything like that to me, I'll be writing my next book from prison.

Maybe that's why Laban did this to Jacob:

> So Laban brought together all the people of the place and gave a feast. But when evening came, he took his daughter Leah and brought her to Jacob, and Jacob made love to her. (Genesis 29:22-23)

I've been to my share of crazy weddings over the years, but I've never seen the groom get so drunk that he didn't notice the bride's dad pulling the *ol' switcheroo* on him. Jacob was livid when, as the story goes, "In the morning, there was Leah!" She wasn't beautiful like Rachel. She was cross-eyed and her body wasn't nearly as fine. On his wedding night, in his drunken state, Jacob had sex with her and, according to custom, Leah was officially his wife.

When Jacob complained to Laban, he literally said, "Why did you deceive (literally *Jacob*) me?" Laban replied like this: "Look here, bud, I don't know how they do things where you come from, but around these parts, we don't give the younger sibling a blessing that belongs to the older sibling." *Ouch.* Remember what Jacob did to Esau? His past had officially caught up to him, and Laban had effectively out-*Jacob'd* Jacob.

Laban agreed to give Rachel away as Jacob's second wife, as long as Jacob agreed to work under Laban for another seven years. Still hopelessly stuck on Rachel, Jacob agreed, and he took her as his second wife.

> Jacob made love to Rachel also, and his love for Rachel was greater than his love for Leah. And he worked for Laban another seven years. (Genesis 29:30)

Leah: *Another Unseen Woman*

At this point, the story's spotlight moves away from Jacob and onto poor, cross-eyed Leah who, unlike her sister Rachel, had never felt loved. It's easy to think how infuriating and confusing the morning after the first wedding was for Jacob, but can you imagine how humiliating and degrading the whole affair must have been for Leah? Her dad had to pass her off as her little sister *just to trick a man into wanting her*.

I imagine Leah held out hope that after she gave herself to Jacob sexually, he might realize that it was really her, and not Rachel, that he wanted all along. In the cold light of day, however, Jacob looked at her and still didn't want her. But God saw Leah much differently.

> When the LORD saw that Leah was not loved, he enabled her to conceive, but Rachel remained childless. Leah became pregnant and gave birth to a son. She named him Reuben, for she said, "It is because the LORD has seen my misery. Surely my husband will love me now." (Genesis 29:31-32)

Leah thought that having a son would make her husband love her. Sadly, she was wrong, and she remained unloved. But that didn't keep her from trying to earn Jacob's affections.

*She conceived again, and when she gave birth to a son she
said, "Because the LORD heard that I am not loved, he gave
me this one too." So she named him Simeon.*

*Again she conceived, and when she gave birth to a son she
said, "Now at last my husband will become attached to me,
because I have borne him three sons." So he was named
Levi. (Genesis 29:33-34)*

After bearing two more healthy sons for Jacob, Leah was still
heartbroken and alone. All that time, Leah had been doing exactly
what Jacob did: she was trying to fill the void in her life with validation and romantic love, but that left her feeling more worthless
and unloved than ever. After getting pregnant for the fourth time,
something happened that changed Leah's outlook. No one knows
exactly why her perspective shifted, but one day, Leah stopped caring
what Jacob thought about her.

*She conceived again, and when she gave birth to a son she
said, "This time I will praise the LORD." So she named him
Judah. Then she stopped having children. (Genesis 29:35)*

When her first son was born, Leah said, "Maybe my husband will
love me now."

After giving birth a second time, she said, "I'm still unloved."

After her third son arrived, she said, "My husband has to want
me now."

But after her fourth son was born, she said, "This time I'll praise
the Lord."

Leah learned her lesson about love. Living for superficial validation and romantic affection will always leave the human heart

101

Living for superficial validation and romantic affection will always leave the human heart unsatisfied.

unsatisfied. In the end, Leah saw the truth about love: it can't be earned with good deeds or coerced by manipulation. She also learned that one man's love pales in comparison to the unconditional love of God. Only God can satisfy our deepest desires. The need Leah thought she felt for Jacob's love was really a much deeper longing for the true love of God.

In some ways, we are all like Leah—living for lesser forms of love, and feeling more alone all the time. All the while, God's love remains, patient and kind, waiting to be loved in return.

CHAPTER FIVE

WHY IS THE BIBLE SO MESSY?

Many well-meaning newcomers to the Bible may feel quickly deflated by the apparent moral ambiguity they find on its pages. They were led to believe that the Bible is the Word of God, and that God is clearly perfect and loving, so they expect the Bible to be loving and perfectly clear. Patient readers may be willing to overlook scriptural discrepancies where historical dates and minor details are concerned, but when it comes to morally unambiguous issues like violence, slavery, and women's equality, it's more than fair to expect the Bible's teachings to be explicitly good.

As we'll see in this chapter, that's not always the case. Many of the stories and laws in the Bible fall painfully short of the moral perfection we might expect from a book that claims to be inspired by the one true God. If God is so perfect, why isn't his Word?

It's complicated.

The Woman Who Dressed Up Like a Prostitute to Trick Her Father In-Law into Making a Baby with Her, Thus Receiving a Double-Blessing from God

I told you it was complicated.

You're not going to believe that the story I'm about to tell you is actually in the Bible, but you can read it for yourself in Genesis 38. It's the story of a man named Judah, the son of Jacob and Leah, grandson of Isaac, great-grandson of Abraham. Judah and his eleven brothers were lauded in Scripture and continue to be lifted up by Jews and Christians as the forefathers of the twelve tribes of Israel.

But here's the thing: generally speaking, the sons of Jacob were not very nice guys. Judah, in particular, was a degenerate, as you will see in the story I'm about to share. Why did Judah turn out that way? I'm guessing it had something to do with how he grew up watching his dad disrespect his mom for being ugly and flirt with her sister instead. Whatever the reasons behind Judah's character defects, one thing is clear: Judah fits right in among other Old Testament protagonists.

The prominent figures throughout the Bible were almost *all* chumps, and I think that's by design. The Bible writers never attempted to cover their protagonists' tracks or to whitewash their filthy deeds. Judah and his brothers were destined by God to form Israel's foundation, but they were, by and large, awful human beings, and the author of Genesis *wanted* us to know just how awful they were.

So here's what happened: In Genesis 37, Judah and several of his brothers were sick of their younger brother, Joseph. Unlike his older siblings, Joseph was Rachel's son, and he was spoiled and full of himself. Judah's frustration with Joseph was perfectly understandable. Who doesn't find their little brother annoying sometimes?

But what did Judah and his brothers decide to do about it? Did they give Joseph a wedgie or replace his toothpaste with Icy Hot, like normal, spiteful siblings would? No—*they sold him to a slave trader for twenty pieces of silver*. And if that weren't bad enough, they proceeded to dip Joseph's coat in lamb's blood before showing it to their father, who recognized the coat and falsely surmised that Joseph must have been torn apart by a wild animal. As Jacob collapsed in grief, neither Judah nor any of the other sons told their dad the truth about what happened. Genesis 37 ends this way:

> *Then Jacob tore his clothes, put on sackcloth and mourned*
> *for his son many days. All his sons and daughters came to*
> *comfort him, but he refused to be comforted. "No," he said,*
> *"I will continue to mourn until I join my son in the grave."*
> *So his father wept for him. (Genesis 37:34-35)*

Can you see how messed up that was? *All his sons…came to comfort him….* Oh, you mean the same sons who sold their brother as a slave, pocketed the money, and then led their dad to believe he was dead? *How sweet of them to come and comfort him.*

The guilt must have weighed heavy on Judah, because Genesis 38 starts with him moving to another country, far away from his father's house. That makes sense; we all try to run from the shame of our past sometimes.

Next, Judah married a foreign girl, and together they had three sons: Er, Onan, and Shelah. When Er came of age and was ready to have a family of his own, Judah arranged for him to marry a young woman named Tamar. But apparently the apple didn't fall far from the tree, because Er was "wicked in the LORD's sight" (Genesis 38:7), just like his daddy, so God struck Er down, leaving Tamar a childless widow.

In those days, the world was harsh and especially unkind to women like Tamar. Women typically survived through their connections to men. A girl depended on her father and brothers for protection and provision until she got married, at which point she relied on her husband. If something happened to her husband, she could be protected by her sons, if she had any.

As a widow with no sons, Tamar was about a half-step away from panhandling, or worse, for the rest of her life. In the Hebrew Bible, however, God established a safety net to protect vulnerable women like Tamar. In this particular instance, God's law commanded that Tamar be given in marriage to her dead husband's younger brother, who then had the duty of procreating with her so she could benefit from the added protections that offspring afforded women in her compromised position.[1]

That collective "eww" you just heard was all the married women reacting to the thought of procreating with their husbands' repulsive little brothers. Just remember: it was a different world back then, and this rule was God's way of looking out for his at-risk daughters.

At first, Judah did the right thing: he gave Tamar in marriage to his middle son, Onan, and he instructed the young man to fulfill his duty by having sex with her and producing a child. But Onan was selfish. He took advantage of the situation by having sex with Tamar, but

> *Onan knew that the child would not be his; so whenever*
> *he slept with his brother's wife, he spilled his semen on the*
> *ground to keep from providing offspring for his brother.*
> *(Genesis 38:9)*

Yep. He just did *that*. People who grew up in Catholic and evangelical churches may have been told that the sin of Onan, or *Onanism*, had to do with masturbation, but Onan wasn't masturbating. He was taking advantage of God's daughter by using her for his own sexual pleasure without offering her the security to which she was entitled according to the Law of God. Can you guess what happened next?

> *What he did was wicked in the LORD's sight; so the LORD*
> *put him to death also. (Genesis 38:10)*

Suddenly, Tamar faced another shadow of uncertainty. In addition to being a widow, twice-over, and still not having any children, people were starting to think she might be a murderer. Her two husbands were apparently young and healthy, but after just a few nights with Tamar, they both ended up dead. So Judah, who was down to his final son, sent Tamar back to her father's house under the pretense that Shelah was pre-pubescent and therefore too young for marriage.

But the author of Genesis tells us what Judah was really thinking:

> *Judah then said to his daughter-in-law Tamar, "Live as*
> *a widow in your father's household until my son Shelah*
> *grows up." For he thought, "He may die too, just like his*
> *brothers." So Tamar went to live in her father's household.*
> *(Genesis 38:11)*

Imagine being so manipulative and self-important that, after losing two sons in rapid succession, you never stop to wonder if maybe what's happening to you is God's righteous judgment for that time you sold your little brother as a slave and then let your father think he got eaten by a wild animal. Or even to stop and consider the possibility that perhaps you've raised a couple of really awful human beings who didn't deserve to live in the first place. Or maybe to stop and feel the slightest bit of empathy for Tamar's precarious situation.

That's just the sort of man Judah was. He expressed no remorse and no self-awareness. He'd been living a lie for so long that he wouldn't know the truth if it undressed right in front of him.

Several years passed—more than enough time for Shelah to come of age—but Judah never contacted Tamar to set the wedding date. One day, Tamar heard that Judah was passing through her town on a business trip, so she disguised herself with a veil and sat down near a busy street. What happened next is truly bizarre:

> When Judah saw her, he thought she was a prostitute, for she had covered her face. Not realizing that she was his daughter-in-law, he went over to her by the roadside and said, "Come now, let me sleep with you."
>
> "And what will you give me to sleep with you?" she asked.
>
> "I'll send you a young goat from my flock," he said.
>
> "Will you give me something as a pledge until you send it?" she asked.
>
> He said, "What pledge should I give you?"
>
> "Your seal and its cord, and the staff in your hand,"

she answered. So he gave them to her and slept with
her.… (Genesis 38:15-18)

Just to recap: after mistaking his estranged daughter in-law—the wife of his two dead sons—for a prostitute, Judah offered to pay her for sex. And Tamar, seeing an opportunity to exact some vigilante justice against Judah for how he had wronged her, went right along with it. She told Judah to make her an offer, and he did: one young goat in exchange for sex with Tamar.

A goat seems like a lowball offer to me, but I confess I am not up to speed on Bronze Age livestock valuations. It didn't matter, because Tamar was clearly not in it for the money (or the goat, as it were); she had something much bigger in the works. Seeing that Judah had no goat in tow, she asked for collateral, and since all that Judah was carrying were his personal effects, she asked him for those, which he freely surrendered. In those days, that was like handing your ID and Social Security card to a random prostitute you just met on the street corner. Why did that matter? Because...*get ready for it*…

"…she became pregnant by him." (Genesis 38:18)

The plot thickens! Unaware of this little development, Judah sent his payment (the goat) via a messenger, but the messenger couldn't find any prostitutes in Tamar's hometown. So he brought the goat back to Judah, who said, "You know what—forget it. I'll just order a replacement ID."

Three months later, Judah heard a rumor that Tamar, who was supposed to be waiting patiently for her marriage to Shelah, had "played the whore" and gotten herself pregnant. Judah was livid. Full of spite and self-righteousness, Judah said, "Bring her out and have her burned to death!" (Genesis 38:24).

But just as Judah's henchmen were dragging Tamar out of her father's house and into the street to execute her, she pulled off the gutsiest, most gangster move in the whole Bible:

> As she was being brought out, she sent a message to her father-in-law. "I am pregnant by the man who owns these," she said. And she added, "See if you recognize whose seal and cord and staff these are."
>
> Judah recognized them and said, "She is more righteous than I, since I wouldn't give her to my son Shelah." And he did not sleep with her again. (Genesis 38:25-26)

How the tables have turned! Judah didn't give Tamar the security that God intended for her to have, so she went rogue. But how severely did that mean, *Old Testament God* punish this young woman for tricking her own father in-law into having sex with her and getting her pregnant? Prepare yourself for another twist: "When the time came for her to give birth, there were twin boys in her womb" (Genesis 38:27).

Remember how I told you that children—and sons in particular—were a blessing from God that represented security for women in Tamar's position? Despite the dubious circumstances surrounding her pregnancy, God gave Tamar a double-blessing of healthy twin boys.

Would you believe me if I told you that's still not the craziest part of Tamar's story? Written nearly two thousand years after the scandal of Judah and Tamar, the Gospel of Matthew opens with the family tree of Jesus:

This is the genealogy of Jesus the Messiah the son of David, the son of Abraham:

> *Abraham was the father of Isaac,*
> *Isaac the father of Jacob,*
> *Jacob the father of Judah and his brothers,*
> *Judah the father of Perez and Zerah, whose*
> *mother was Tamar." (Matthew 1:1-3, emphasis*
> *added)*

Maybe this God isn't who you thought he was.

Think for a moment about all the things you've heard people say about the God of the Bible. How have you heard Christians, in particular, describe the character of God? Is the God of Tamar and Judah consistent with the God so often represented by smug, sanctimonious Christians? Not exactly.

This God rewarded a woman, twice-over, for deceptively bedding her own father in-law. And if that were not enough, God also chose to write Judah and Tamar into humanity's most important family tree.

Maybe this God isn't who you thought he was.

Maybe the Bible is better than advertised.

Messy Like a Starry Night

The first step in learning to love the Bible is understanding how your perspective affects what you observe in Scripture. Imagine yourself in New York's Museum of Modern Art, standing in front of Van Gogh's masterpiece *The Starry Night*. Hoping to understand the method to Van Gogh's madness, you lean toward the painting as far as you can without incurring the guard's wrath and, raising a magnifying glass to your face, you zero in on a single, isolated section of this great work of art. What do you see?

Chaos. Messy, formless, seemingly random chaos. You see nothing but yellow, blue, and black smudges with no apparent rhyme or reason. Feeling underwhelmed, you fix your gaze on another section of the painting, only to find an entirely different kind of chaos: dots upon dots upon more dots. You expected to find more beauty and cohesion in Van Gogh's work up-close, but the closer you get, the uglier it looks and the less sense it makes.

Shaking your head, you slide the magnifying glass into your pocket, trying to understand what you just saw. You step back for one last look, and there it is: the masterpiece you love. From this distance, what you failed to see up-close comes into focus: all the ordinary, ugly parts work together to make something extraordinarily beautiful. You glance around the room at other works by Van Gogh, Pissarro, Monet, and Cassatt, and at last, you realize the true genius of the Impressionists. They understood something that most people miss: up close, life on earth can seem like meaningless noise, but from a distance, it's perfection.

Astronauts in outer space often experience the same phenomenon when they reach orbit and look back at planet Earth for the first time. Many of these highly-trained interstellar scientists report entering a state of absolute mental clarity called the Overview Effect,[2] which leaves them feeling overwhelmed by the mystery of existence and the sheer size of humanity's spatial home. The sixth man to ever walk on the moon was Apollo 14 astronaut Edgar Mitchell, who said,

"The beauty of seeing earth as a planet as opposed to being down here among it is a wonderful experience."[3]

What a difference perspective makes! In the minutiae of day-to-day life, earth can seem like a lackluster, burdensome place. Those who have taken a cosmic "step back" to see the bigger picture would beg to differ. When astronaut Nicole Stott returned from the International Space Station, she said,

> "You start out with this idea of what it's going to be like, and then when you do finally look at the earth for the first time, you're overwhelmed by how much more beautiful it really is.... It's this dynamic, alive place that you see glowing all the time."[4]

A common theme among astronauts who have experienced the Overview Effect is the feeling that life on earth is a gift that should never be wasted or taken for granted. Consider the profound reflections of NASA astronaut Ron Garan who, after laying eyes on earth from outside the International Space Station, was struck by the unlimited possibilities that perspective can afford us:

> It was as if time stood still, and I was flooded with both emotion and awareness. But as I looked down at the Earth—this stunning, fragile oasis, this island that has been given to us, and that has protected all life from the harshness of space—a sadness came over me, and I was hit in the gut with an undeniable, sobering contradiction. In spite of the overwhelming beauty of this scene,... I couldn't help thinking of the nearly one billion people who don't have clean water to drink, the countless

number who go to bed hungry every night....Part of this is the realization that we are all traveling together on the planet and that if we all looked at the world from that perspective we would see that nothing is impossible.[5]

Whether you're looking at a work of art, planet Earth, or the Bible, your point of view will determine what you see.

How could something as messy as this polluted planet, replete with pain and suffering, inspire someone to say, "Nothing is impossible"? It's all about your perspective. Whether you're looking at a work of art, planet Earth, or the Bible, your point of view will determine what you see. Read up-close with a magnifying glass, the *Good Book* contains some very bad things. Zoom in on the wrong parts, and you'll likely feel underwhelmed, if not disgusted. But a change in perspective changes everything. Sometimes you have to step back to see the beauty.

Do You See This Woman?

I admit, it's not always easy to spot the beauty in the Bible. Some of the stories about women in the Bible, for example, make me sick to my stomach. At first glance, it seems inexcusable to many skeptics that women were subjected to such awful treatment in a book that is purported by Christians to be holy. But take a step back, and you'll see the whole picture: each one of the nightmare narratives in Scripture contributes to a greater, more beautiful story God wants to tell about the daughters he loves so much.

After God promised Abraham and Sarah (a.k.a. Abram and Sarai) they would have children, even though they had been barren, they tried for months to conceive. Nothing happened, so Sarah began to think she was the problem, and in Genesis 16, she decided to take matters into her own hands.

> *Now Sarai, Abram's wife, had borne him no children. But she had an Egyptian slave named Hagar; so she said to Abram, "The Lord has kept me from having children. Go, sleep with my slave; perhaps I can build a family through her."…*
>
> *He slept with Hagar, and she conceived. (Genesis 16:1-2, 4)*

I hardly know where to begin with a story this twisted. Was Sarah really so desperate that she would just offer another woman to her husband? Could she not see how impossibly awkward this situation would become, especially if things went according to plan and Hagar got pregnant? Did she really believe that God needed her help making his promise come true? Whatever she was thinking, it backfired:

> *When [Hagar] knew she was pregnant, she began to despise her mistress. Then Sarai said to Abram, "You are responsible for the wrong I am suffering. I put my slave in your arms, and now that she knows she is pregnant, she despises me. May the Lord judge between you and me."*

> *"Your slave is in your hands," Abram said. "Do with her*
> *whatever you think best." Then Sarai mistreated Hagar; so*
> *she fled from her. (Genesis 16:4-6)*

In case you're keeping score at home, Hagar now resents Sarah, who resents Abraham, who is just doing his best to stay out of trouble. But the real victim here is Hagar, who finds herself pregnant, penniless, and without a home. Sadly, this plight befell women all too often in the ancient world. Without a father, husband, or brother to protect her, a woman's options dwindled to panhandling, prostitution, or starvation. This was especially true for a foreign, female slave like Hagar.

After she flees Sarah's abuse, however, something unforeseen happens in the wilderness. God finds Hagar, alone and in distress, and he comforts her. Imagine Hagar's surprise when God tells her it will be safe for her to go back to Abraham and Sarah, and when he assures her that she and her unborn son are part of his great plan, too. Her baby was not some mistake to be discarded; he would become Ishmael, the father of the Arab nations. Look how Hagar responds to God's kindness:

> *She gave this name to the LORD who spoke to her: "You are*
> *the God who sees me," for she said, "I have now seen the*
> *One who sees me." (Genesis 16:13)*

For someone who probably felt unseen for most of her unfortunate life, the gift of being seen by God was a revelation. Those who patiently and faithfully study the most brutal Bible stories involving women will begin to see a common thread. Women in the ancient world were largely invisible, and even though no one else saw them,

God always did. Even though in some ancient cultures women were disposable, God refused to allow women—or their stories—to be so carelessly discarded.

Dismembered by One, Remembered by All

The most horrific story in the entire Bible is found in the Old Testament book of Judges. In the nineteenth chapter, we encounter an unnamed Levite, or Israelite priest. This particular priest had a concubine, which is a slightly more refined way of saying *sex slave*, but he got the impression that she was cheating on him, so he sent her back to her father's house.

The priest got lonely after a few months so he decided to reclaim his concubine. He approached her father and asked for permission to repossess her, and her dad was more than happy to send his little princess back into sex slavery. *Father of the Year*, he was not.

On their way back to the priest's house, they lost track of time and the sun set on them as they passed through an unfamiliar town. That was bad news. There were no flashlights or cellphones or police officers; nighttime travelers were dead meat. Lucky for them, a local villager took them in, but as they were getting ready for bed, a violent mob of men began to bang on the doors of the man's house. Before opening the door, the villager asked them what they wanted, and they shouted back, "Bring out the man who came to your house so we can have sex with him" (Judges 19:22).

To be clear, they wanted to gang-rape the priest. Scholars and historians have suggested that this sort of behavior wasn't unheard of in those days. Gang-rape was, and continues to be in some parts of the world, a weapon of terror and intimidation. It was their way of sending a message to an outsider like this priest that he was not welcome on their turf.

The hospitable villager refused to meet the thugs' demands; instead, he offered to send out his young daughter and the priest's concubine for the men to rape instead. When the rapists refused the offer, the priest took his concubine and threw her out the front door anyway, and the men all took turns beating and raping her outside of the house until dawn.

At dawn, the woman crawled back toward the house, but she collapsed on the porch before she made it through the front door. A while later, the priest got out of bed and prepared to head home without even looking for the girl. When he opened the front door and stepped outside, he looked down and saw her lying there. He said, "Get up, let's go," but she didn't answer him. She was probably already dead. This is how the story ends:

> When he reached home, he took a knife and cut up his
> concubine, limb by limb, into twelve parts and sent them into
> all the areas of Israel. Everyone who saw it was saying to one
> another, "Such a thing has never been seen or done, not since
> the day the Israelites came up out of Egypt. Just imagine! We
> must do something! So speak up!" (Judges 19:29-30)

And that's it. The end.

I'm sure you have questions, and so do I. Questions like *What the hell did I just read?* and *Isn't that from a Stephen King novel?* and *Why in God's name is this story in the Bible?*

This is precisely the sort of material I used to point out when I was a cynic to state my case about the insanity of the Bible. If you ever, for any reason, want to shut down a conversation with a mouthy Christian, I recommend asking him why the Word of God includes the story of a priest who dismembered his sex slave and FedEx'd her body parts to the twelve tribes of Israel. They'll have no idea what to do with that.

When you get past the trauma of this story, however, and you begin to ask some deeper questions, you might see what I've come to appreciate most about the Old Testament: its brutal honesty. I used to assume that, by including this story in the Bible, the authors of Scripture were endorsing the Levite's bad behavior. In my cynicism, I thought: *If there are concubines in the Bible, then the Bible is OK with concubines. If women are harmed in the Bible, then the Bible is OK with harming women.*

But do you really believe the people who wrote and pieced together the Bible thought to themselves, "This story stays because of its moral contributions to the canon"? Of course not! The whole theme of *Judges*, in particular, is found in the oft-repeated refrain: "In those days there was no king in Israel; all the people did what was right in their own eyes" (Judges 21:25 NRSV). The whole book is a condemnation of Israel's own reckless disdain for the Law of God.

The same holds true for this story. Look once more at how the people responded when they heard what the priest had done: *Just imagine! We must do something! So speak up!*

The ugliness in Scripture doesn't diminish the beauty of God; if anything, God inspired the messiest parts of the Bible to offer a stark contrast to his holy perfection. The Levite believed his concubine was disposable, but he couldn't have been more wrong. To God, she is indispensable. Men like the Levite often forget people like her, but God never forgets. God remembers. To the Levite, she was property to be used and destroyed. To God, she is a daughter to be treasured and loved.[6]

She Told Him the Whole Truth

In the New Testament there is another story about a woman who, though all but forgotten by men, was remembered by God. These events took place in Capernaum where, as Jesus and his entourage pulled their boats ashore, a swarm of people surrounded them, hoping to get close to Jesus. Among the crowd was a very important man named Jairus, who was one of the city's top religious officials. Jairus made his way through the mob to reach Jesus, and when he did,

> He pleaded earnestly with him, "My little daughter is dying.
> Please come and put your hands on her so that she will be
> healed and live." So Jesus went with him. (Mark 5:23-24)

So Jairus led Jesus toward his home while the disciples did their best to keep the crowd at bay, but Mark tells us that one person managed to slip through their human barricade. We don't know her name, just her story:

> And a woman was there who had been subject to bleeding
> for twelve years. She had suffered a great deal under the
> care of many doctors and had spent all she had, yet instead
> of getting better she grew worse. When she heard about
> Jesus, she came up behind him in the crowd and touched his

cloak, because she thought, "If I just touch his clothes, I will be healed." (Mark 5:25-28)

This woman fascinates me. After bleeding vaginally, and uncontrollably, for twelve years, and spending her life savings on doctor bills, her condition only got worse. Sometimes while reading Bible stories I stop and try to imagine what these people were really like. This woman was probably a young adult, in her 20s or 30s, and with pale skin and a frail gait due to her prolonged blood loss. Bible scholars have suggested that she was childless because of her reproductive condition, which raises the likelihood that she was unmarried or divorced because bearing children was a wife's primary responsibility in her context.

Bleeding uncontrollably was an especially big deal in ancient Hebrew culture because of the strict Old Testament laws prohibiting casual contact with body fluids. According to Leviticus 15, vaginal bleeding made a woman unclean, and no man was allowed to go near a menstruating woman. It's safe to assume that, for twelve long years, no one had touched this woman, and she was probably forced by local authorities to move out of her family's home and to live outside the city walls. The day she met Jesus, she was a sick, penniless, hopeless social outcast; her life was a painful, lonely struggle. Her only hope was this construction worker-turned-rabbi she'd heard so much about. So she threw a *Hail Mary* pass: she covered her sunken, anemic face and shoved her way through the crowd, getting close enough to touch his clothes.

And she was instantly healed. I wonder what that was like.

Can you imagine bleeding for so long that *not bleeding* felt new?

It's strange though, right? Why did she touch Jesus's "clothes"?

What she actually touched was a tassel, called a *tzitzit*, worn by devout Jews over their robes to signify their family or tribal identity. More than likely, Jesus's *tzitzit* identified him as a descendant of King David, which was a pretty big deal, and by law, no "unclean person"— like someone who'd been hemorrhaging for over a decade—was allowed to touch a man's *tzitzit*, especially when that man is a healer who is on his way to save the life of a VIP's daughter.

Jesus felt it when she touched his *tzitzit*, so he turned and asked his disciples who touched him. But they were so stressed out by the crowds that they get a little snarky with Jesus:

> *"You see the people crowding against you," his disciples*
> *answered, "and yet you can ask, 'Who touched me?'"*
> *(Mark 5:31)*

Modern translation—*Dude, look around. Who hasn't touched you?! Keep moving!*

As Jesus scanned the crowd to find out who had touched him, he looked down at the ground and laid eyes on the poor woman who was at once grateful and terrified. On the one hand, she felt *amazing* for the first time in twelve years, but on the other, she'd broken about fifty rules in the Bible just to get to Jesus. Biblically speaking, she was unclean, and so was everybody she touched in her condition. How many people do you think she touched as she elbowed her way through the mob that day? Even more importantly, she made Jesus unclean too, which meant that he should not be allowed to go and heal Jairus's daughter. As if that weren't enough guilt, she also touched a man's *tzitzit*, something only immediate family members were allowed to do.

Jesus could have sentenced her to die for this. Her life was literally in his hands. Instead, Jesus and the woman shared one of the sweetest, most elegant exchanges in all of Scripture:

> *Then the woman, knowing what had happened to her,*
> *came and fell at his feet and, trembling with fear, told him*
> *the whole truth. He said to her, "Daughter, your faith has*
> *healed you. Go in peace and be freed from your suffering."*
> *(Mark 5:33-34)*

She told Jesus the *whole truth*. I'm not completely sure what that means, but I'm guessing this woman wasn't just saying she was sorry for being unclean and touching all those people. I think it means she told Jesus her *story*. Keep in mind, that was a noisy scene and a raucous crowd; in order for Jesus to hear her story, he must have bent down and gotten real close to her. Can you see him kneeling, listening as this terrified, ostracized woman told him *everything* she'd been through for the previous twelve years?

By this point in the story, it's safe to assume that some people in the crowd had recognized her as the unclean, untouchable woman who lived outside of town. As word spread and tempers flared over this woman who has defiled Jesus by illegally touching him, he spoke. And what was the first word Jesus said to her?

Daughter.

This is the only time in all four of the Gospels that Jesus called anyone his *daughter*, so why *her*? First, to absolve her of her guilt for touching him. Do you remember who was allowed to touch a man's *tzitzit*? Immediate family only. By calling this woman his daughter, Jesus was telling her accusers to back off. Second, Jesus called her daughter to *assure* her that, even though she'd been through hell on earth, her heavenly Father saw her. And third, Jesus referred to this woman as his daughter to *adopt* her.

He absolved her. He assured her. And then he adopted her. That is what Jesus came to do for all of us, because that is who God *is* and, throughout all of Scripture, that is what God *does*.

Eat Your Dang Cream Taters

Absolution, assurance, and adoption: that's the grace of God, in brief. Throughout my childhood, I remember seeing real grace in action just by following my grandmother around. She was a tough, Southern woman. She was so tough, in fact, that she refused to let her grandchildren call her "Grandma" or "Granny" like normal kids would. If any of us ever dared call her *Granny*, she would scowl at us and say, "Do I look like a 'Granny' to you?"

She could be scary, so we consented to call her by her name: Virgie. Virgie *Merle*. You have to be a tough woman to survive a middle name like Merle, and she was as fierce as they come. Virgie grew up during the Great Depression of the 1930s, the daughter of a Methodist preacher and a homemaker. Like many in her generation, Virgie spent most of her life working too hard, relaxing too little, and saving as much money as possible ... but never in the bank, because according to Virgie, banks couldn't be trusted.

Virgie spent her entire life in a remote Texan town called Red Lick. Most people there were related somehow, which made courtship a little tricky, but everybody knew everybody, and everybody felt safe. Except Virgie, who slept with a hatchet under her pillow every night and drove her Dodge Ramcharger through the piney woods of northeast Texas with a loaded revolver in the glove compartment. "A helpless Christian girl can't be too cautious," she would quip in her southern drawl.

Virgie lived a hard life. She married a part-time dairy farmer-turned-truck-driver-turned-preacher, and before long they had a daughter, Anita Sue. When Anita Sue was barely two years old, she died of an allergic reaction to penicillin. Virgie later had three more children—all girls—and all three of them grew up wrongly believing that they, too, were allergic to penicillin, because Virgie told every doctor who came near them to keep that "poison" away from her babies.

When the girls were 16, 11, and 7, their daddy—my Grandpa Ray—had a heart attack and dropped dead, and suddenly, Virgie was a single mother. She was down, but not out, and soon enough she found a way to move her family forward. When she was forty-two, and while holding down a full time job and raising three girls, Virgie went to night school and earned her master's degree in special education. She went on to teach students with special needs in public schools for over a decade.

More than anything else, Virgie loved to cook for her family. Her southern cuisine was legendary, and her specialties included lard-fried pork chops, made-from-scratch dinner rolls, black-eyed peas with bacon, collard greens with bacon, baked beans with bacon, and basically anything else with bacon. But the dish Virgie was known for was her mashed potatoes—she called them "cream-taters"—which had no nutritional value whatsoever, but none of us cared. When I was a kid, and our whole family gathered at Virgie's house to eat some of those rich, creamy, perfectly whipped carbo-hydrates, all my worries melted away like the countless sticks of real butter Virgie used in every batch.

When I was sixteen, one of my older cousins, James, got into some trouble. Like Virgie, James had survived a difficult upbringing. When he was still a baby, his dad served two tours in Vietnam, and like a lot of soldiers who fought in that war, he left home a good man with a bright future, and came back shell-shocked, paralyzed by irrational fears, anxiety, and addiction. He was unable to hold any job for very long; James and his siblings grew up in poverty.

Virgie was so proud of James when, at age 19, he landed a good job in the business office of the local Community College. Then one day, after working there for almost a year, James was abruptly termi-nated. Within a few hours, the news had spread throughout our family that James had been caught stealing thousands of dollars from the business office. College officials were threatening to press charges unless he reimbursed the school immediately, but James had already spent the money that he had stolen.

Virgie was the only person James knew with that kind of cash laying around the house—literally, it was right there in her mattress—so he went to her for help. Initially, Virgie said no; she was inclined to believe that James would benefit in the long-run if he suffered the short-term consequences of his actions. After thinking it over for a few days—and making James sweat a little—she gave him the money that he needed, but it was very clear to everyone that she wasn't happy about it.

The next day, all of us grandkids went over to Virgie's for a sleepover which, under normal circumstances, would have been quite the party. That night, however, Virgie's house had all the warmth of a maximum security prison. As she made dinner, she stirred the batter as if it had disappointed her and threw pots and pans around as though they owed her thousands of dollars. I can't be sure if Virgie intended to make James feel bad, but I know that every clashing sound coming out of that kitchen felt like another ringing indictment against my poor cousin.

At last, dinner was served, and as we all started to dig in, James awkwardly sat there, not eating. I don't know if he was sick to his stomach because of what he did, or if he thought that Virgie would interpret his restraint as some kind of self-imposed punishment. Whatever the case, Virgie did not appreciate the sentiment. After a few excruciating moments, Virgie got up from her chair, walked around the table to where James was sitting, and hastily began shoveling mounds of food onto his dinner plate.

James' voice shook when he said, "No, Virgie, please, it's fine. Really, I'm not that hungry." Virgie threw down the serving spoon and turned toward her thieving grandson. She pointed her bony, arthritic finger at his face and yelled, "Eat your dang cream-taters, James!" He choked those potatoes down like his life depended on it.

Neither James nor any of the rest of us understood what was really going on, what Virgie's potatoes represented at that particular place and time. We all thought Virgie was angry and James was being punished. But her insistence wasn't punitive; it was restorative. She wasn't mad; she was desperate. The thought of losing her wayward grandson was more than she could handle. *Eat your dang cream-taters* was an invitation back to her table. Those potatoes were grace.

Many people see God the same way James saw Virgie that night—angry and vindictive—and they look at the Bible like James looked at those potatoes—like something they must consume or else. But what if God isn't mad? What if he just loves us? And what if the Bible isn't punitive? What if that's how grace works sometimes? And what if God's invitation to read his word was never meant to be a bitter pill, but simply an invitation back to his table?

One night, as his enemies conspired to arrest and eliminate him, Jesus hosted a dinner party to celebrate the Passover with his disciples and closest friends. Also present were Judas, who sold Jesus out, and Peter, whose cowardice would be on full display in the hours that followed. Their presence at Jesus's table is a welcome reminder to sinners like me that, no matter what we've done, the invitation to dine with God is still open. And when I allow my sin and shame to convince me to walk away from his table, it pains him to let me go without.

The Bible is messy because real life is messy.

The Bible is messy because real love is messy.

The Bible is messy because God is love.

CHAPTER SIX

IS THE BIBLE RACIST?

Annyeonghaseyo!

After a fifteen-hour flight, I gathered my carry-on and stumbled to the front of the aircraft, where flight attendants welcomed me to their homeland with a cheerful Korean *hello*. After receiving a fellowship to study East Asian religions for the summer, I took my first steps on foreign soil at the age of nineteen. Excited and afraid, I managed to fight through the fevered frenzy at baggage claim and the chaos at customs before exiting the airport and hailing my first-ever taxicab. I opened the door, gave the driver a friendly nod, and said what I'd been instructed to say:

Ewha changmoon juseyo!

At least that's what I *thought* I'd been instructed to say. For my readers who don't speak Korean, that's how you say "Please window university." Ninety minutes later, and twenty-five thousand *South Korean won* poorer, I finally arrived at Ewha University, the world's largest women's university. My summer exchange program was co-ed, so I was one of only eight men on a campus of nearly twenty thousand women. To make matters more interesting, upon getting to know my fellow foreign exchange students, I discovered that our program was specifically intended for Korean-American students.

As you can probably tell from my picture on the back cover and my Germanic last name, I am not Korean-American. I quickly called the Director of International Studies at my college and asked her if I was in the right place. That's when she decided to tell me that she gave me the fellowship only because no Korean American students had bothered to apply. *Now you tell me.*

My first day in Seoul, I met someone who changed my life. I first laid eyes on him while taking a walk around the campus. He towered over the student body, with his giant arms stretched wide. The look on his face was resolute, but kind. Bearing marks on his hands and feet, he was at once familiar and foreign to me. I knew I was looking at a statue of Jesus, but not the same Jesus I worshiped back home. My Jesus was thinner, friendlier, and his face looked more like mine. This Jesus looked serious and stout, and his facial features were clearly Asian.

I must have stood there, staring at Korean Jesus for a solid half hour. I had yet to outgrow the cultural limitations of my ultra-rural, East Texas upbringing, and my teenage, underdeveloped frontal cortex was slow to process what I was seeing.

Do people here worship a different Jesus?

Do they not know what Jesus really looked like?

I failed half my classes that summer, but the experience shaped me for the better. Every Sunday morning, I visited a different church, and I witnessed the faith of Korean Christians as they passionately worshiped Jesus. Something I learned that summer stuck with me through thirteen years of agnosticism and anti-Christian indignation: Jesus cannot be contained by any one race, language, ethnicity, or nationality.

The Bible and White Supremacy

Here's a question for you: how many biblical authors were white men?

Christianity's critics confidently cast the Bible as a tool used by white men to found empires and beat people into submission in some vile, patriarchal conspiracy. No one can deny the historical fact that far too many atrocities have been perpetrated in the name of Christianity, and far too often, white men have been to blame. The facts around the Bible's origins, however, do not support the narrative that it perpetuates racist patriarchy.

The Bible's original geographic, cultural, and literary contexts were anything but monolithically masculine. The fact that it was written entirely by men does little to resolve the questions that matter. What sort of men were they? What kinds of oppression did they have to overcome? What were their views of women and minority groups? How have their writings contributed to the liberation and equality of historically oppressed people?

Yes, the authors of the Bible were probably all male, but gender is the only demographic category they all had in common. King Solomon, the author of Ecclesiastes, Song of Songs, and most of Proverbs, was born into wealth and power. Moses, who wrote most of the first five books of the Old Testament, was an at-risk orphan. Paul, author of thirteen New Testament letters, appears to have been raised with some privilege, as evidenced by his stellar education and his Roman citizenship. Peter, on the other hand, was an illiterate fisherman who became the most influential figure in first-generation Christianity. It is particularly remarkable that, even in a time far less respectful of women than our culture is today, two books—Ruth and Esther—are dedicated entirely to women's stories, and many other women played essential, if not heroic, roles in the most important book ever written. Those who accuse the Bible of racism and misogyny conveniently leave out details like these. Why? Because when your narrative matters more than the truth, facts hurt.

The answer, by the way, is none of them.

The total number of white male Bible writers is zero.

That racists and sexists use the Bible as a tool proves nothing about the Bible.

Diversity is so important to the God of the Bible that, from the very beginning, he insisted on it.

It merely proves, yet again, that racists and sexists are tools.

Diversity is so important to the God of the Bible that, from the very beginning, he insisted on it. Consider the very first commandment God gave to Adam and Eve:

> *God blessed them and said to them, "Be fruitful and*
> *increase in number; fill the earth and subdue it."*
> *(Genesis 1:28)*

Just to be clear: the first rule handed down by God in Scripture was not "Worship me and only me!" It wasn't a "Thou shalt not…" God's first rule for humans was "Go have sex. Lots and lots of sex. Keep having sex until you *fill the earth.*"

So, God wanted the whole earth full of people. He wanted Bedouin tribes learning to live under the hot, desert sun; he delighted in Eskimos building igloos to survive Siberian winters. God wanted city centers where human ingenuity and creativity can thrive, and he smiled as farmers learned to tame the overgrown wilderness. "Fill the earth" was God's mandate for diversity; from the start, he intended for human beings to scatter, inhabiting every continent, adapting to every climate, evolving into a rainbow of races, and creating quirky, contrasting cultures.

The Allure of Uniformity

One of Scripture's oldest stories may also be its strangest: the mysterious account of the Babel tower in Genesis 11. The story goes like this: in primeval times, all human beings belonged to one, uniform culture:

> *Now the whole world had one language and a common*
> *speech. (Genesis 11:1)*

The people were aware that God wanted them to fill the earth, but they were afraid of being scattered, so they decided to stick together and build a single city for everyone to call home. At the city's center, they built a massive tower, which God did not appreciate because the tower symbolized humanity's rejection of his original order to fill the earth with sex and babies. The people preferred the safety of the same over the broad diversity that God intended.

And who can blame them, really? From our faith communities to our residential neighborhoods, humans appear to be hooked on homogeneity. Throughout history, our nation-states have been almost exclusively monochromatic, as have most of our religions. Against this backdrop, the Bible makes the audacious claim that God's design for us has forever been manifold variation; he will not tolerate the standardization of a singular social identity.

> So the LORD scattered them from there over all the earth,
> and they stopped building the city. That is why it was called
> Babel—because there the LORD confused the language of
> the whole world. From there the LORD scattered them over
> the face of the whole earth. (Genesis 11:8-9)

This is the Bible's explanation for how multiple races, cultures, and languages expanded and evolved to the ends of the earth. Something about the diversity of humankind makes God smile. Some might look at the Bible and say, *But didn't God choose one ethnic group to be "his people" exclusively? Doesn't that prove that God loves some cultures more than others?* No—the Old Testament is crystal clear that God called the Hebrews for the purpose of reaching and claiming people from every tribe and nation to be his children. That's why in Genesis 12, 15, and 22, God promised Abraham he'd be the father of many nations, not just one:

The LORD had said to Abram, "Go from your country, your people and your father's household to the land I will show you.

> *"I will make you into a great nation,*
>> *and I will bless you;*
> *I will make your name great,*
>> *and you will be a blessing.*
> *I will bless those who bless you,*
>> *and whoever curses you I will curse;*
> *and all peoples on earth*
>> *will be blessed through you." (Genesis 12:1-3, emphasis added)*

[The LORD] took him outside and said, "Look up at the sky and count the stars—if indeed you can count them." Then he said to him, "So shall your offspring be." (Genesis 15:5, emphasis added)

"Through your offspring all nations on earth will be blessed, because you have obeyed me." (Genesis 22:18, emphasis added)

Lending further credence to God's affinity for diversity, the remaining thirty-eight Old Testament books keep spinning the same record by promoting unlikely, foreign heroes like Rahab (a Canaanite prostitute) (Joshua 2:1), Ruth (a Moabite widow) (Ruth 1:4), Caleb (a mighty Kenizzite warrior) (Numbers 32:12), and Cyrus (a Persian king) (Ezra 1:1-2). The Hebrew prophets often warned the people not to forsake the global vision God cast to their forefathers. Through the prophet Isaiah, for instance, God reminded the Israelites that his love extended to non-Jews (Gentiles) as well:

> *"It is too small a thing for you to be my servant*
> > *to restore the tribes of Jacob*
> > *and bring back those of Israel I have kept.*
> *I will also make you a light for the Gentiles,*
> > that my salvation may reach to the ends of the
> > earth." *(Isaiah 49:6, emphasis added)*

When God's people failed to heed his desire to bless all the people of the earth, he scattered them again, just as he had done at Babel. The theme of gathering, scattering, and gathering again repeats in the Bible like Bill Murray's wakeup song in *Groundhog Day*. Whenever God's people gathered safely in Hebrew-only havens, he scattered them. Why? Because there is no risk in such cocoons of complacency, and thus no room for faith. There is no flavor in homogeneity, and the Bible's God is anything but vanilla.

Scattered

Fast-forward to the days when Jesus walked the earth. His disciples loved being in their little *Jesus Club* together. It made them feel special and important. And what guy wouldn't want to hang out with Jesus? He told the best stories and could do the craziest magic tricks. If Jesus had allowed it, I'm certain those twelve guys would have kept him all to themselves. But Jesus knew that a storm was brewing in Jerusalem, and that he would soon be arrested, beaten, convicted, and crucified. So this is what he told them:

> *"A time is coming and in fact has come when you will*
> *be scattered, each to your own home. You will leave me*

all alone. Yet I am not alone, for my Father is with me."
(John 16:32)

Why do you suppose Jesus said this? Was he giving himself an *I'm not alone* pep talk? Unlikely. The real reason Jesus told his disciples that he would never be alone was because he knew they would soon be scattered and lonely. He was arrested just a few days after saying these words, and as he predicted, his terrified disciples were scattered. As they all ran for their lives in different directions, I imagine all of them recalling Jesus's promises, whispering to themselves, "I am not alone, for my Father is with me."

Several weeks later, God brought the scattered disciples back together in the New Testament book called *Acts of the Apostles*. In what reads like a reversal of the Babel tragedy, believers from diverse parts of the world gather in the same place and suddenly are able to understand each other as if they're speaking the same language. This is the story of the first official church service:

> *Utterly amazed, they asked: "Aren't all these who are*
> *speaking Galileans? Then how is it that each of us*
> *hears them in our native language? Parthians, Medes*
> *and Elamites; residents of Mesopotamia, Judea and*
> *Cappadocia, Pontus and Asia, Phrygia and Pamphylia,*
> *Egypt and the parts of Libya near Cyrene; visitors from*
> *Rome (both Jews and converts to Judaism); Cretans and*
> *Arabs—we hear them declaring the wonders of God in*
> *our own tongues!" Amazed and perplexed, they asked one*
> *another, "What does this mean?"*
>
> *Some, however, made fun of them and said, "They have had*
> *too much wine." (Acts 2:7-13)*

It was a party, but it didn't last very long. Remember: God's plan isn't just for a few of us to enjoy his love among friends. So just a few chapters later, the believers were scattered again:

> On that day a great persecution broke out against the church in Jerusalem, and all except the apostles were scattered throughout Judea and Samaria....
>
> Those who had been scattered preached the word wherever they went. (Acts 8:1, 4)

I made my final edits to this book as the world learned to cope with the casualties and consequences of COVID-19. Right now, everyone I know feels isolated and afraid. Most businesses have shuttered temporarily, if not permanently. Churches have closed down, too. Worship services have been reduced to pastors awkwardly broadcasting with iPhones in our living rooms. All of this is an attempt to starve the virus by what the experts are calling "social distancing."

Social distancing is the closest that most modern, western Christians have ever come to being scattered like the first Christians were. For extroverts like me, it might as well be hell on earth; I've tried to fill the void with everything from meditation to potato chips, but so far, nothing has worked. Introverts seem to be doing fine, but their cats can't wait for them to go back to work so they can have the house to themselves again. The schools are closed; parents are working from home while also keeping our kids from going all "Cain and Abel" on each other.

Scattering is hard to do. In fact, nobody really practiced social distancing until we found out that Tom Hanks got the virus. The next thing we knew, they canceled March Madness and the Tokyo

Olympics, and people who happened to be aboard a Carnival cruise received, um, extended vacations.

There are silver linings in our scattering, however. This week alone, I've worshiped with Christians from New York and New Zealand to South Africa and South Dakota through the power of the World Wide Web. Even though my church has been unable to gather for over seven months, with no end to this crisis in sight, we have more than tripled our reach with people online. For the first time in my life, almost every church in America was empty on Easter Sunday, but so was the tomb of Jesus, so his followers still had cause for celebration, even in our scattered state.

If nothing else, this crisis is a welcome reminder that our faith is at its best when we're taking risks in unfamiliar territory. The real church isn't what happens in our buildings as we gather on Sundays in mostly homogeneous congregations. The church is all of us, from every nation and race, speaking different languages, finding our common ground in Jesus Christ. One day the world will go back to normal; I hope churches in America never do.

The First Black Christian

The first Christians were olive-skinned Jews from the Middle East; it took about a decade's worth of breakthroughs for God to convince the Hebrew Christians that his vision was much bigger than the nation of Israel. One of the earliest and most important developments is recorded in the eighth chapter of the Acts of the Apostles, when Philip, a follower of Jesus, met an Ethiopian government official on the Gaza Road:

> *And there was an Ethiopian, a eunuch, a court official of*
> *Candace, queen of the Ethiopians, who was in charge of*
> *all her treasure. He had come to Jerusalem to worship and*
> *was returning, seated in his chariot, and he was reading*
> *the prophet Isaiah. And the Spirit said to Philip, "Go over*
> *and join this chariot." So Philip ran to him and heard him*
> *reading Isaiah the prophet and asked, "Do you understand*
> *what you are reading?" And he said, "How can I, unless*
> *someone guides me?" And he invited Philip to come up and*
> *sit with him. (Acts 8:27-31 ESV)*

This encounter should not have happened. Philip was Jewish; this man was a Gentile. Philip was an Israelite; this man was Ethiopian. Philip (like every other Christian at the time) was olive-skinned; this man was black. For these reasons and more, Philip had no business associating with the likes of this dark-skinned foreigner. So why did he do it? Because God told him to!

Even though most believers are really nice people who like to think that everyone belongs with Jesus, Christian prejudice is as old as Christianity itself. If we're honest, we all have biases that inform our understanding of who really belongs in our churches. Some of our prejudices are based on Scripture, while others stem from our political leanings and personal experiences. We all make some assumptions about who belongs with God and who doesn't. The first Christians, for instance, were all in agreement that black, Ethiopian Gentiles did not belong with Jesus.

Riding high in the royal chariot, this Ethiopian eunuch was on his way back home to northeast Africa. Although he was not Jewish, he had visited Jerusalem to worship Yahweh, the God of Israel. The most likely explanation for his trip is that he was sent there on a diplomatic mission by his boss, the Ethiopian queen.

Eunuch isn't a word you hear every day, but the plight and status of these castrated servants were well-known in the ancient world. Most eunuchs were orphaned at a young age because of the poverty and/or death of their parents. They were typically purchased as slaves by wealthy patrons, who had them castrated around the age of 8. Without the benefits of anesthetics or antiseptics, castration was unimaginably traumatic for boys. Some reports on the castration of male slaves in the ancient world suggest that as few as 20 percent of castrated boys survived the procedure.[1]

The ones who survived became extremely valuable slaves who were entrusted with some of their masters' most sensitive jobs. It's not hard to understand why. If you were a king in the ancient world, and you had a harem full of gorgeous, young wives, whom would you choose to stand guard and protect them? Your strongest, most virile soldier, or the slave with no testicles? And who would you hire to taste your food before you ate it to make sure it hasn't been poisoned? Some poor sap who has a wife and six kids depending on him, or a eunuch, who had no one to go home to? The eunuch in this story was in charge of the Ethiopian queen's treasury because she could trust him. Since he had no competing interests or ambitions, the royal bank was safe with him.

As valuable as eunuchs were to their masters, they did not belong with Jesus, at least not according to first-century Jews and first-generation Christians. Their Bible, the Old Testament, clearly states that a castrated man cannot belong to the congregation of God's people.

No one who has been emasculated by crushing or cutting
may enter the assembly of the LORD. (Deuteronomy 23:1)

I'll be real with you; I don't know why the Bible ever sought to exclude guys with crushed genitals. It would seem to me that having your genitals crushed is punishment enough. Nevertheless, it's in there, and I'm sure God and Moses had their reasons. While visiting the Jerusalem Temple to pay homage to God, this man was certainly kept at arm's length by Jewish officials.

Eunuchs were easily identifiable by their elongated necks and high-pitched voices. When Philip heard the eunuch reading from the Book of Isaiah, he knew exactly what kind of person was in that chariot. Philip, however, was compelled by something far more powerful than prejudice, so when the eunuch asked him to explain the prophet's words, the two men from different worlds sat, side by side, to unpack the story of Jesus together.

> *Now the passage of the Scripture that he was reading was this:*
>
> > *"Like a sheep he was led to the slaughter*
> > > *and like a lamb before its shearer is silent,*
> > > *so he opens not his mouth.*
> > *In his humiliation justice was denied him.*
> > > *Who can describe his generation?*
> > *For his life is taken away from the earth."*
>
> *And the eunuch said to Philip, "About whom, I ask you,*
> *does the prophet say this, about himself or about someone*
> *else?" Then Philip opened his mouth, and beginning with*
> *this Scripture he told him the good news about Jesus.*
> *(Acts 8:32-35 ESV)*

Put yourself in that eunuch's place for a minute. Try to imagine hearing the story of Jesus with the ears of this man who didn't belong. How would a story whose hero never gets married and never has children appeal to you? What would it mean to you to hear a story about a savior who was humiliated and rejected? How might you relate to a God who bore the scars of a punishment he didn't deserve, if you were a eunuch who bore the humiliating scars of a curse you didn't deserve? What happened next would change the church, and the world, forever:

> And as they were going along the road they came to some water, and the eunuch said, "See, here is water! What prevents me from being baptized?" And he commanded the chariot to stop, and they both went down into the water, Philip and the eunuch, and he baptized him. And when they came up out of the water, the Spirit of the Lord carried Philip away, and the eunuch saw him no more, and went on his way rejoicing. (Acts 8:36-39 ESV)

In his tell-tale, high-pitched voice, the eunuch asked if anything could stand in his way of being baptized. It was not a rhetorical question. He really wanted to know if the same factors that precluded him from worshiping inside the Jerusalem Temple also might disqualify him from belonging with Jesus.

The truth is that any one of those issues were enough to prevent the eunuch's baptism. Baptism has always been a huge deal for Christians; it's the primary rite of initiation into the church. The one who is baptized in Christ *belongs* to Christ. If baptized, this man would become the first Ethiopian Christian, the first African Christian, the first Gentile Christian, the first castrated Christian, and of course, the first black Christian.

That's why few people would have blamed Philip for avoiding responsibility in response to the eunuch's question. He could have echoed the tepid sentiments of a polite, indecisive preacher, "You know, I need to pray about this for a few days, so let me get back to you." He could have channeled a politician's empty rhetoric and said, "Let me take this matter to the Church Council in Jerusalem, and if we have the votes, I'll gladly baptize you." Or he could have spoken like a Methodist and said, "I'll look into forming a Committee on the Baptism of Castrated Africans. I'll let you know what is decided, but it's a committee, so it might take a few years."

Philip said none of those things, thank God. Instead, he stopped the chariot and walked toward the water, with the awestruck eunuch a few steps behind. They walked into the water as perfect strangers: a Jew and a Gentile, an Israelite and an Ethiopian, an olive-skinned disciple and a black-skinned eunuch. Everything changed, however, the moment Philip plunged his companion's mutilated body beneath the surface. The tally of things they held in common grew only from zero to one, but their sole commonality was more than enough to shape two strangers into brothers, eternally bound by the blood of Jesus.

The eunuch asked Philip, "What prevents me from belonging with Jesus?" By baptizing his new baby brother, Philip gave the most eloquent, compassionate response: *nothing*.

Five chapters later in Acts, Luke introduces a Christian named Simeon in a very awkward way:

Now in the church at Antioch there were prophets and teachers: Barnabas, Simeon called Niger, *Lucius of Cyrene, Manaen (who had been brought up with Herod the tetrarch) and Saul. (Acts 13:1, emphasis added)*

If you look closely, you'll notice that Simeon is the only person listed with a nickname. The word *niger* (pronounced *nee-jer*) literally meant "black guy." So, Simeon was black. This is where things get awkward, but only because in post-Enlightenment, post-slavery, post-segregation America, we rightly frown upon the use of race-based labels, stereotypes, and even nicknames. Life in first-century Mesopotamia was different, I suppose, because Simeon didn't seem to mind the other Christians calling him "the black guy."

What's more interesting is how this nickname is a pretty solid clue that Simeon was the only black Christian at the time. Why else would they call him that? I imagine it started like this:

Christian A: "Have you met Simeon yet?"

Christian B: "No, which one is he?"

Christian A: "Simeon, the black dude."

Christian B: "Oh the black dude, yeah!"

And thus Simeon became *Niger*. Here's the crazy part: multiple first- and second-century Christian sources suggest that Simeon, a.k.a. Niger, was the eunuch whom Philip baptized. A church father named Irenaeus connected the dots for us around AD 180:

> This man {Simeon Bachos the Eunuch} was also sent into the regions of Ethiopia, to preach what he had himself believed, that there was one God preached by the prophets, but that the Son of this [God] had already

> made [His] appearance in human {flesh},…and had
> been led as a sheep to the slaughter; and all the other
> statements which the prophets made regarding Him.[2]

It is very likely that Simeon, this fraction of a man who was barely more than a slave, this man whose emasculated body was condemned by Scripture, this man with the voice of a woman, this black man who spent his life on the outside, looking in, this lovesick man who asked, "What prevents me from being baptized?" emerged from his baptismal waters and took the gospel to Ethiopia, introducing Jesus and his gospel to the African continent.

Today there are more Christians in Africa than there are people in the United States. Experts predict that Africa will soon overtake the United States as Christianity's epicenter; by 2025, there will be six hundred, thirty-three million African Christians. Six hundred, thirty-three million people who can trace their soul-saving, personal relationship with their Creator all the way back to one man, sitting in his chariot, wondering what could prevent him from belonging with God.

Black and Christian in America

African-American author James Baldwin once said, "To be a Negro in this country and to be relatively conscious is to be in a state of rage almost all the time."[3] For many Black Americans, this country's historic realities of racism and oppression of black people is still a fresh wound that can't be healed by simply recalling the story of the first black Christian. There is too much history, too much pain, and too little empathy to merely move along without listening to the stories that Christians of color are telling.

I've had several conversations about race with fellow believers on the *Maybe God Podcast*. In the first season, an African American pastor, Rev. Rudy Rasmus, wept as he told me that it's harder to be Black and Christian today in America than it has ever been.[4] That is a shocking statement, especially when you consider that Rudy grew up in the waning years of codified segregation in the South. How could being Black and Christian in America be more difficult now than it was back then?

Black Christian friends have told me that it's harder now because, whereas in the days of segregation it could be said that white Christians never heard the stories that Black Christians were telling, now the pain and trauma Black Americans have experienced for generations is on full display in the form of books, art, movies, and YouTube videos.

Even so, to many Black Christians in America, it feels as though either some of their white siblings are not listening or they are denying the reality of black people's pain. Many white Christians, myself included, have been quick to point to statistics as evidence that our society is no longer racist, or not as racist as it used to be. Hoping to be helpful, people say things like, "Things are better than they've ever been for black people in America," "What about reverse racism?," and "Stop talking about the police—black-on-black crime is the real problem here," seemingly oblivious to the heavy burdens that many Black Americans carry due to the trauma of many generations of subjugation and violation.

In another *Maybe God* episode, Dr. Esau McCaulley, a professor of New Testament at Wheaton College, responded to the *whataboutisms* that some white Christians offer up in response to the Black experience:

African Americans have said for centuries that racism is a systemic problem. We've said for decades upon decades, that the way in which we're policed is a problem. And so now these videos are occurring and you have a choice. You can rethink the ways which you failed to take seriously African American Christian testimony, or you can find evidence that supports your worldview....

There's probably not a more consistently disbelieved Christian community who are consistently disbelieved by other Christians than African Americans saying to their white brothers and sisters, "This is what's happening to us in America." And we are consistently being told, "No, it's not." *With video!*[5]

So, is the Bible a friend or a foe in the fight against bigotry? While we cannot deny that racists have used the Bible as a weapon of oppression, they've done so by choosing a few isolated verses at the expense of Scripture's call to do justice and to set the captives free. From Frederick Douglass's conviction to Dr. King's dream, the movement to liberate black people was always built on biblical truths.

As our culture continues to wage war on the racist demons of our past and present, many people wonder what hope we have for reconciliation.

During the months I've spent writing this book, protesters have filled America's streets in response to the violent deaths of George Floyd, Breonna Taylor, Ahmaud Arbery, and other Black Americans. As our culture continues to wage war on the racist demons of our past and present, many people wonder what hope we have for reconciliation. Will better politics fix us? Will saying certain slogans right what's wrong? Will the right hashtags on social media heal our nation? It's unlikely.

Dr. McCaulley wrote a column for the *New York Times* in which he equated the rage that so often surfaces in the Psalms to the rage that filled America's streets in 2020.[6] In the Psalms, King David wrote, "LORD, ... how long shall the wicked triumph?" (Psalm 94:3 KJV). Through the Psalms, the Jewish people cried out for God to exact judgment upon their enemies in neighboring Gentile kingdoms. Elsewhere in the Old Testament, however, God discourages ethnic divisions between Jews and Gentiles:

> *"It is too small a thing for you to be my servant*
> > *to restore the tribes of Jacob*
> > *and bring back those of Israel I have kept.*
> *I will also make you a light for the Gentiles,*
> > *that my salvation may reach to the ends of the*
> > *earth." (Isaiah 49:6)*

In the same Old Testament, we find the call for God's judgment upon our enemies *and* a vision for restoration and reconciliation. How can both of these things be in the Bible? How can two seemingly competing ideas be reconciled? According to McCaulley, it's the cross.

"That tension is resolved on the cross. The cross allows me to say *both*, 'Sin is utterly serious,' *and* 'There's a path towards forgiveness.' And so I try to . . . not simply explain away black concerns for justice by saying the cross makes us one. Forgiveness doesn't actually require the lack of truth-telling or the lack of transformation. . . . What the gospel does, it says there's more than revenge and so it can't simply be, 'I take revenge upon you' [because] when I take revenge upon you, that revenge is disproportionate, which creates its own grievances. And then that party rises up and it's this cycle of violence and revenge. And so . . . the cross breaks the wheel."[7]

That's the difference Jesus makes. He can't be contained by any category or culture. He won't be restricted by any race or religion. He is big enough for everyone to belong and strong enough to bring us together. How did the Bible gain a reputation for being oppressive and racist? I can't be sure. But when you cut through the noise and go straight to the source, it's clear: according to the Bible, everyone who wants to belong, belongs.

Show me a more diverse movement than the church.

Show me a more inclusive message than the gospel.

Show me a better story than the Bible.

You can't. It doesn't exist.

The Bible stands alone.

CHAPTER SEVEN

CAN WE TALK ABOUT LEVITICUS?

Leviticus is the third book in the Hebrew Bible and is known for its various and sundry lists of rules for holy living. Because so many of the laws handed down in this book don't seem to apply to our modern lives, Leviticus has become synonymous with irrelevance. Christians tend to think of Leviticus like that one crazy cousin you keep around, but only because you're related and it seems like the right thing to do. You invite him to dinner, but when he turns up on the news for doing something stupid and somebody says, "Hey isn't that your crazy cousin?" you do your best Simon Peter impersonation:

I do not know that man!

Yeah, that's pretty much how we treat Leviticus. It's the last book we turn to when defending the Bible, but it's the first place

Christianity's critics go when debunking the Bible. Back when I thought I was too smart to be a Christian, one of my favorite pastimes was poking fun at believers by pointing out the wildest verses I could find in Leviticus. Verses like:

> *"You will eat the flesh of your sons and the flesh of your daughters." (Leviticus 26:29)*

> *"A woman who … gives birth to a son will be ceremonially unclean for seven days.… If she gives birth to a daughter, for two weeks the woman will be unclean." (Leviticus 12:2, 5)*

> *"If a man or woman develops a sore on the head or chin, the priest will offer a diagnosis. If it looks as if it is under the skin and the hair in it is yellow and thin, he will pronounce the person ritually unclean. It is an itch, an infectious skin disease." (Leviticus 13:29-30 MSG)*

As a clergyman, can I just say how thrilled I am that the job description for my profession has changed over the years? I want nothing to do with your gross, hairy head sores, thank you. Verses like these are the reason why you've probably never heard anyone say, "I believe the Bible is the Word of God because of something I read in Leviticus." According to Google, the most popular online searches starting with the words "Leviticus is…" include "Leviticus is wrong," "Leviticus is hard to read," "Leviticus is hate speech," and "Leviticus is BS."

You get the idea. People don't like Leviticus. But do we have good reasons to cast the Bible's third book aside? I'm not so sure.

Context Clues

Anyone who ever paid attention in ninth-grade English class knows that, before deciding what you think about any piece of literature, you first need to understand the context in which it was written. People who unilaterally dismiss Leviticus often do so under the guise of intellectualism or social woke-ness, but all I see is laziness and fear. I recognize it, because before I surrendered my life to Jesus, I perfected that brand of conceited, fearful snark about the Bible.

We all suffer from a condition that C. S. Lewis called *chronological snobbery*,[1] which is the blind assumption that an earlier culture, belief system, moral code, or way of life is automatically inferior to the present day *just because it's older*. If you don't believe you're a chronological snob, just search on the internet for *1980s hair bands* or *Zach Morris cell phone* and try not to laugh at those old dorks whom people used to idolize. See? Deep down, we're all chronologically conceited.

We do the same thing with a book like Leviticus when we look back and dismissively laugh it off. To understand this book, we have to imagine, as much as possible, what life must have been like for a fledgling network of malnourished former slaves wandering the Judean wilderness over three thousand years ago. For many generations, they had been dehumanized as slaves in Egypt:

> The Egyptians became ruthless in imposing tasks on the
> Israelites, and made their lives bitter with hard service in
> mortar and brick and in every kind of field labor. They
> were ruthless in all the tasks that they imposed on them.
> (Exodus 1:13-14 NRSV)

Nobody in Egypt cared about the Israelites,[2] but as we've seen throughout this book, God always sees the people who are invisible to the powers that be. He told Moses:

> *"I have observed the misery of my people who are in Egypt;*
> *I have heard their cry on account of their taskmasters.*
> *Indeed, I know their sufferings, and I have come down to*
> *deliver them from the Egyptians, and to bring them up out*
> *of that land to a good and broad land, a land flowing with*
> *milk and honey." (Exodus 3:7-8 NRSV)*

On several occasions, through his messenger Moses, God commanded Pharaoh to free the slaves, but the Egyptian monarch refused. In order to get Pharaoh's attention, God sent a series of plagues upon the Egyptians: *frogs, lice, gnats, flies, lightning,* and *hail.*

Not gonna lie, that sounds a lot like Houston, but I digress.

The plagues grew more severe, but Pharaoh wouldn't listen until God finally ran out of patience and sent the last plague: the death of every Egyptian firstborn son. In the wake of this tragedy, Pharaoh relented and allowed the Hebrew slaves to go free…*for about five minutes*, at which point he changed his mind and ordered his troops to pursue the rogue slaves and return them to Egypt.[3]

Nevertheless, the Israelites escaped, but as it turns out, leaving was the easy part. From the second half of the book called Exodus all the way through the end of the book called Judges, the Israelites struggled to find a way to survive as an independent community with no king, no land, and no shared history other than the chains they wore in Egypt.

I assume that the lives of nomadic herdsmen have always been tough, but things were extra harsh throughout Mesopotamia during the years following the Israelites' escape from Egypt. By studying ancient pollen residue, archaeologists have confirmed that a massive drought led to a famine about the time the Israelites were adjusting to life after slavery.[4] During that time, nomadic tribes like the Israelites lost as much as half their population. Infant mortality rates throughout the region topped fifty percent. The limited supplies of food and water led to localized violence as roving bands of warlords took whatever they could by force.

Facing the possibility of death in the desert, some of the Israelites actually *complained* about having lost the security they enjoyed as slaves:

> *The Israelites said to them, "If only we had died by the*
> *LORD's hand in Egypt! There we sat around pots of meat*
> *and ate all the food we wanted, but you have brought us*
> *out into this desert to starve this entire assembly to death."*
> *(Exodus 16:3)*

This world of hardship and regret was the
context that gave rise to Leviticus.

This world of hardship and regret was the context that gave rise to Leviticus. Believe it or not, all those crazy rules were God's way of giving the struggling Israelites a path toward hope and survival as they wandered aimlessly through the wilderness. Most people today who dismiss Leviticus because it's too harsh and arbitrary are simply showing their deeply entitled snobbery.

Leviticus Is a Love Story

When you put yourself in the sandals of those men and women who were just trying not to die and to keep their kids alive, while honoring the God who loved them, the purpose behind this book comes into focus: Leviticus is a love story.

Love is the reason why so much of Leviticus is about sanitization. Love is why God told the Israelite leaders: You must distinguish between clean and unclean, and teach the Hebrews (Leviticus 10:10-11, paraphrased). To us, it sounds like rigid religion; to the Hebrews trying to stay alive, keeping clean things away from unclean things meant survival.[5]

Love is why God gave the people strict rules about what to eat, and what not to eat. It wasn't arbitrary or manipulative; there were always deeper reasons behind the food laws. Pigs, for example, are disgusting creatures that will eat absolutely anything. Pigs will consume their own dead offspring if given the chance. Did you know the mafia used to dump their victims' corpses in pig pens because pigs consumed *everything*—bones and all—thus eliminating all incriminating evidence? Maybe that's why God said, "Y'all really shouldn't eat those things."

Shrimp, which were also forbidden in Leviticus, are basically the pigs of the sea. They're filthy. Other animals that the Israelites were not allowed to eat included bats, rats, vultures, hyenas, weasels, and catfish. Most of the forbidden creatures were scavenging bottom-feeders that survived by consuming the carcasses of other dead animals.

God wasn't just being mean when he outlawed bacon and bats. He was looking out for his kids because he wanted them to live. Why? *Love.*

Love is why God told the Israelites to be extra careful with skin diseases and infections (Leviticus 13:1-44). Communicable illnesses could have spread and wiped out the whole community overnight, so God handed down quarantine guidelines for the sake of love:

> *"Anyone with such a defiling disease must wear torn clothes, let their hair be unkempt, cover the lower part of their face and cry out, 'Unclean! Unclean!' As long as they have the disease they remain unclean. They must live alone; they must live outside the camp."* (Leviticus 13:45-46)

Seven months ago, I would have said this sounds like cruel and unusual punishment. Just because you're a little concerned about getting sick, you're going to force someone into isolation, to cover their face, and to look all messy and disheveled? But COVID-19 has revived the Leviticus instinct within us all. My hair has been unkempt since March 2020. People now refer to social distancing, wearing a mask, and washing your hands as *acts of love.*

And that is exactly the point Leviticus makes. All this time, we've been making fun of Leviticus, and now we're living it.

Is Leviticus Homophobic?

But let's be real: nobody is actually *bothered* by levitical laws about pigs, mildew, and hairy open oozing sores, right? In fact, the only reason anyone ever mentions any of those rules is when a Christian insists that gay sex is a sin. The conversation usually goes something like this:

Woke Wendy: *Can you believe that in twenty-first-century America there are still people who think that sex between people of the same gender is wrong?*

Christian Carl: *Yeah, actually, that's what I believe.*

Woke Wendy: *What?! Why do you hate gay people so much?*

Christian Carl: *Hmm, I don't. I just believe what the Bible says about sex and marriage.*

Woke Wendy: *Oh you mean Leviticus? I guess you eat shrimp and bacon though, huh?*

Christian Carl: *I mean yeah, because in the New Tes—*

Woke Wendy: *I knew it. You're a hypocrite and you hate gay people!*

Christian Carl: *[sigh]*

Here's the thing about most of the sex laws in Leviticus: as open-minded as we think we are in the twenty-first century, almost everybody today would agree with almost every sex law in Leviticus. To prove my point, I'll list all of the prohibitions from the infamous eighteenth chapter of Leviticus, and I'll place a checkmark beside every rule with which virtually everyone today *agrees*:

Verse 6: No one is to approach any close relative to have sex. √
Verse 7: Do not have sex with your mother. She is your mother. √
Verse 8: Do not have sex with your step-mother. √
Verse 9: Do not have sex with your sister. √
Verse 10: Do not have sex with your granddaughter. √
Verse 11: Do not have sex with your step-sister. √
Verse 12: Do not have sex with your aunt. √

Verse 13: Don't have sex with any of your aunts. √

Verse 14: I mean it, you guys. No aunts! √

Verse 15: Don't have sex with your daughter in-law. √

Verse 16: Do not have sex with your sister in-law. √

Verse 17: Do not have sex with a mom and daughter at the same time. √√

Verse 18: Don't have sex with your wife's sister. √

Verse 19: Don't have sex during menstruation.[6]

Verse 20: Do not have sex with your neighbor's wife.√

Verse 21: Do not sacrifice your children to Molek.[7] √

Verse 22: Don't have same-sex relations.

Verse 23: Do not have sex with animals. √

If you're keeping score at home, the most notorious, supposedly sex-negative chapter in the most scandalous, supposedly backward book in the Bible contains seventeen rules about sex, and we all absolutely agree with fifteen of them. So how did Leviticus earn its reputation for being so wrong about sex? It all comes back to the LGBTQ+ revolution that has taken place over the last thirty years in our culture.

LGBTQ+ people and their sexual expressions went from *alternative* to *mainstream* so quickly that we forget what a different conversation we were having in this country until just a few years ago. Consider this: in 1987, 85 percent of Americans said that sexual relations between two adults of the same sex is wrong, compared to only 11 percent who said it's perfectly fine.[8] By 2017, 70 percent of Americans said homosexuality should be accepted by society, while only 24 percent said homosexuality should be discouraged.[9]

For many young adults, it's unthinkable that, in the twenty-first century, a future president of the United States would say that he believes "marriage is between a man and a woman," and that, unlike the civil rights afforded to people of color, marriage is not a civil right that is guaranteed to people of all sexual orientations. While explaining his anti-gay-marriage convictions, he said, "We have a set of traditions in place that I think need to be preserved." Explaining how his traditional views on marriage were informed by his faith, he said, "For me as a Christian, [marriage] is also a sacred union. God's in the mix." Even as the world around us raced toward sexual progressivism, our country elected a president who has said all of those things—and more—while speaking out against gay marriage.

And that president's name was Barack Obama.[10]

I'm not here to slam President Obama. While I'm no longer a Democrat, I do confess that I've missed the feeling of looking up to a president who's stayed married to the same woman and never paid porn stars any hush money and never weekended with the likes of Jeffrey Epstein. Those were the *days*, I tell ya'.

The only reason for mentioning Obama is to remind you how quickly support of all LGBTQ+ people and expressions has become all but mandatory in our culture today. Whereas in generations past, when coming out as gay was enough to get you fired, beaten, or worse, in 2021, anything short of vocal, unflinching support of all things LGBTQ+ will likely get you in some big trouble. At this rate, it's only a matter of time before the traditional, biblical view of sex and marriage will be deemed illegal hate speech and Christians who are seeking to honor Scripture will be forced to make a choice between legal consequences and eternal ones.

Sex and the Rest of Scripture

Leviticus is not the only Bible book that points to sex between a man and a woman in marriage as the only God-honoring form of sexual expression. In addition to the many prohibitive passages in Leviticus 18 and 20, various parts of Scripture condemn all sorts of sexual sins, from premarital sex and orgies to adultery and having sexual fantasies about someone else's spouse (Exodus 22:16-17; 1 Corinthians 6:18-20; 1 Thessalonians 4:3-5; Matthew 5:27-28). To most people these days, this looks like a case study in unhealthy sexual repression so common among world religions.

In reality, however, in terms of sexuality, the Bible is the most progressive and sex-positive sacred text the world has ever seen. I know you probably don't believe that, but humor me for the next few paragraphs and you'll see what I mean.

We've established by now that the Bible is full of rules that God has handed down from on high, but do you recall the first rule God imposed upon the first human beings?

> God blessed them and said to them, "Be fruitful and increase in number; fill the earth and subdue it." (Genesis 1:28)

Another way of saying "Be fruitful and increase in number" is "go have a TON of sex and fill the earth with babies." And from that point on, despite what you may have heard, the scriptures are full of sex-positivity. The fact that a book called *Song of Songs*[11] was included in the Bible at all never ceases to amaze me. If the men who wrote the Bible books and approved the canonization of Scripture were truly sexually sheltered and archaic, *Song of Songs* would never have seen the light of day. Bible scholar Tremper Longman explains:

> The role of the woman throughout the Song {of Solomon} is truly astounding, especially in light of its ancient origins. It is the woman, not the man, who is the dominant voice throughout the poems that make up the Song. She is the one who seeks, pursues, and initiates. {In Song 5:10-16} she boldly exclaims her physical attraction ["His abdomen is like a polished ivory tusk, decorated with sapphires..." (14)].... Most English translations hesitate in this verse. The Hebrew is quite erotic, and most translators cannot bring themselves to bring out the obvious meaning.... This again is a prelude to their lovemaking. There is no shy, shamed, mechanical movement under the sheets. Rather, the two stand before each other, aroused, feeling no shame, but only joy in each other's sexuality.[12]

You probably figured this out already, but the woman in *Song of Songs* wasn't really saying her lover's *abdomen* is like a polished ivory tusk. She meant...you get it, right? Don't make me say it. I told you the Bible is full of surprises.

The sex-positivity spills over into the New Testament in some surprising ways as well. The apostle Paul, who is assumed by many to have been Christianity's stickiest stick in the mud, had some extremely nuanced views on sex, especially for the first-century world in which he lived. When instructing Christian husbands and wives how to honor Jesus in their marriage, he dropped this unexpected piece of advice:

> *The husband should fulfill his marital duty to his wife, and likewise the wife to her husband. The wife does not have*

authority over her own body but yields it to her husband. In the same way, the husband does not have authority over his own body but yields it to his wife. Do not deprive each other except perhaps by mutual consent and for a time, so that you may devote yourselves to prayer. Then come together again so that Satan will not tempt you because of your lack of self-control. (1 Corinthians 7:3-5)[13]

Most people who possess some vague, secondhand knowledge of Paul's writings would likely expect him to tell wives that they have no authority over their own bodies. But very few people are aware that Paul ever told Christian men that our wives have control and authority over our bodies. Think about that for a second. Paul is telling a bunch of first-century brutes that, if they had a long day at work and just want to throw back a sixer and watch the game, but their wives are in the mood for some lovin', then it's time for lovin'. *No excuses, fellas. God said so.* That's in the Bible!

In this passage, Paul's message about sex in marriage is clear: do it, do it often, take a break to pray or whatever, and then do it some more.

If Sex Is So Good, Why Are Christians So Afraid of It?

Still, there can be no denying that Christians have earned our reputation for being sexually backward. St. Augustine (AD 354-430) was the first Christian leader ever documented to have taught that sex for any purpose other than reproduction is a sin. In a Sunday sermon, St. Jerome (AD 347-420) once told the men of his church that any husband who is too passionate a lover with his own wife is himself an adulterer.[14] Every man in St. Jerome's church then leaned over to his wife and said, "I guess I better repent, if you know what I mean," to which every wife responded with a chuckle, "I don't think you have anything to worry about, dear."

Throughout the majority of church history, Christian leaders have been guilty of amplifying the dangers of sexual sins while simultaneously going silent on other, equally sinful acts like pride, greed, and anger. We've also judged some sexual sins, such as homosexual expression, more harshly than premarital sex and pornography use, to name a couple. Instead of resorting to defensive *whataboutisms*, Christians would serve the Kingdom well to simply acknowledge our regrettable track record of hypocrisy where sexual sin is concerned.

With that said, it's also worth mentioning that some Christians have emphasized sexual sins with the best of intentions. Some, for example, have noticed that the Bible seems to warn readers about the devastating power of misplaced sexual desire with more frequency, and with greater urgency, than many other common sins. Passages like this one appear to further validate the concern many Christians have about the exponential harm that sexual sin, in particular, can cause:

> *Flee from sexual immorality. All other sins a person commits are outside the body, but whoever sins sexually, sins against their own body. Do you not know that your bodies are temples of the Holy Spirit, who is in you, whom you have received from God? You are not your own; you were bought at a price. Therefore honor God with your bodies. (1 Corinthians 6:18-20)*

In recent years, many Christians have felt prompted to hyper-analyze and overemphasize sexual sins because they feel like our culture's moral foundations are crumbling beneath our feet. I try not to be an alarmist, but it's hard to deny that, when it comes to the normalization of sexual identities and expressions that were long-assumed to be detrimental in the Western world, we've wandered into uncharted territory. In one recent study of adults involved in a romantic relationship, 85 percent of participants reported watching internet pornography in the past six months (including 98 percent of men),[15] and the average age of first exposure to internet pornography is eleven.[16] Children under ten account for 22 percent of online porn use among people eighteen and younger.[17] One in four American adults would be willing to enter or consider an open relationship (such as *polyamory* or *swinging*),[18] and while 32 percent of adults under 30 would be willing to enter or consider an open relationship, seventeen percent of those in this age category have already been in at least one.[19]

Everyone is entitled to his or her own opinions about whether these trends are ultimately good or bad. Even if you disagree with the traditional sexual ethics of biblical Christianity, however, it should come as no surprise when you see or hear Christians challenging the ever-evolving, anything-goes sexual ethos of our secular society.

I've counseled church members in every stage of life: insecure teens, wide-eyed undergrads, frustrated singles navigating the perils of Tinder, engaged couples preparing for marriage, married couples careening toward divorce, divorced people recovering from marriage, and the list goes on. Over the past few years, more than ever before in my lifetime, sexual sins—compulsive or addictive behaviors, betrayal, dysfunction, and other forms of sexual brokenness—are presenting an existential threat to many, if not most, of our individual souls, as well as our romantic relationships. I believe much of this pain is enabled by churches and pastors who have chosen, for the sake of a false sense of peace and inclusiveness, to remain silent about sexual sin. Those of us in positions of Christian leadership must stand up and teach biblical Truth about these issues for the well-being of those in our communities.

"But Jesus Never Condemned Homosexuality"

Many who want to advocate for greater inclusion of more sexual identities and expressions expect Christians to acknowledge the fact that, while Leviticus and some of Paul's letters appear to call out gay sex as sinful, Jesus himself never explicitly condemned LGBTQ+ sexual expressions. They concede that Jesus addressed lust and adultery, but they also point out that he didn't go out of his way to define God-honoring marriage and sexual intimacy strictly in terms of one man and one woman. If, as Christians claim, Jesus is the ultimate authority on all things, why are we going out of our way to denounce sexual behaviors that he didn't think were worth mentioning?

While I understand the reasoning behind this very common question, it lacks precision. First, Jesus actually did address sexual ethics several times throughout his life on earth. In his famous *Sermon on the Mount*, for example, he said that directing sexual desire at someone who is not your spouse is on par with adultery

(Matthew 5:27-28). On several other occasions, Jesus lifted up the sacred nature of a male body becoming one with a female body:

> "Haven't you read," he replied, "that at the beginning the
> Creator 'made them male and female,' and said, 'For this
> reason a man will leave his father and mother and be
> united to his wife, and the two will become one flesh'? So
> they are no longer two, but one flesh. Therefore what God
> has joined together, let no one separate." (Matthew 19:4-6)

In addition to this popular pericope about a man and wife becoming *one flesh*, Jesus often illustrated his teachings using wedding imagery, usually referring to himself as the bridegroom and the church as his bride.[20] This image is repeated throughout the rest of the New Testament, from Paul's admonishment for husbands to love their wives "as Christ loved the church" (Ephesians 5:25), to John's vision of the future union of Christ and his bride—the church—in the fascinating book called Revelation:

> "Let us rejoice and be glad
>   and give him glory!
> For the wedding of the Lamb has come,
>   and his bride has made herself ready."
>   (Revelation 19:7)

Why does any of this matter to the question of Jesus's views on sexuality and marriage? Because it's quite clear that Jesus held views on marriage and sexual expression that were in step with the values of traditional Judaism that were rooted in the Levitical Law. His silence on issues like gay marriage and same-sex relations was in no way due to the fact that he was more permissive than Christians are today. If anything, Jesus's standards for sexual goodness were far loftier than ours. Remember, this is the same Jesus who said this about the rules in the Hebrew Bible:

> *"Do not think that I have come to abolish the Law or the Prophets; I have not come to abolish them but to fulfill them." (Matthew 5:17)*

Some Christians have argued that people in biblical times, including Jesus, had no concept of lifelong, loving, same-sex relationships because the only types of "homosexual relations" depicted in Scripture were abusive ones.[21] Prominent New Testament scholar N. T. Wright disagrees with this assumption:

> As a classicist, I have to say that when I read Plato's *Symposium*, or when I read the accounts from the early Roman empire of the practice of homosexuality, then it seems to me they knew just as much about it as we do.... They knew a great deal about what people today would regard as longer-term, reasonably stable relations between two people of the same gender. This is not a modern invention, it's already there in Plato. The idea that in Paul's day it was always a matter of exploitation of younger men by older men or whatever... of course there was plenty of that then, as there is today, but it was by no means the only thing.[22]

As a friend and pastor to many LGBTQ+ people, I've often wished the Bible offered some clear loophole for same-sex romantic relationships and marriages to be recognized and blessed by the church, but it just isn't there.

My friend David is a brilliant author and scholar at Oxford University who has studied under N. T. Wright. After coming out as a gay man at age fourteen, he became an anti-Christian LGBTQ+ activist throughout his high school and college years. One night, David was hanging out at a bar in the famous gay quarter of Sydney, Australia, when a young woman asked if she could pray for him. He said yes, and as she prayed, David was shocked by some powerful, warm presence that came over him. He didn't know what it was at the time, but he later identified it as the Spirit of God. That night, under the neon lights of an Australian gay bar, David became a follower of Jesus.

Since then, David has done some difficult, diligent work to discern God's will for his life, including his sexuality. After many months of prayer, reflection, and Bible study, he came to the conclusion that his sexual orientation as a gay man has always been a God-given part of who he is, and that's probably not going to change in this life. David doesn't believe that being attracted to people of the same sex is any more or less sinful than any other sexual orientation is; for all of us, it's what we do with our sexual orientation that counts. So David decided to commit to a life of celibacy for the sake of Jesus and his kingdom, and now he spends much of his time sharing his story with secular gay activists all across the world.

In his incredible book, *A War of Loves*, David shares the story of a time when he spoke at a university outside of London as part of an interfaith discussion about gay marriage. Although the gathering was advertised as a "safe space," David remembers feeling anything but safe. When the time came for him to speak, the room was tense and David's heart was pounding. Then he spoke:

> "Well, this may not be popular in this room," I said, "but as a gay...celibate Christian, I do not believe gay sexual expression is right for me."..."I believe God made our bodies.... The fact that God created human beings with two sexes reveals he values both the diversity and unity of human persons, not because he wants to condemn LGBTQI people!"..."For Christians, marriage between the male and female sexes takes on a deeper meaning only when we understand the relationship of Jesus, who's the Bridegroom, and the church, who's his bride."[23]

As far as I'm concerned, no one speaks with more clarity and authority on matters pertaining to sexuality and the Bible than David does. Let's not forget the chosen sexual expression of Jesus and the apostle Paul who, like David, were committed to celibacy. People like Jesus, Paul, and David Bennett have bigger fish to fry with their time on earth than mere romantic entanglements. They've got real love to share and lost souls to save.

We Christians have a lot of work to do on these issues. Generally speaking, we have responded to these issues in one of two ways:

- We lay down the gauntlet and tell the world that, not only is gay sexual expression a sin, *being a gay person is a sin, period*, regardless of whether or not you pursue those desires. This is what I call the *Sorry You're All Going to Hell* doctrine.

- Because we are nice, we never talk about it until it all blows up in our faces, and then we realize we have to pick a side, so we choose to be nice and approve of all gender and sexual expressions, not on principle but just because we are so nice. This is what I call the *Chocolate Easter Bunny* doctrine because it's sweet and cute on the outside but inside, it's empty.

Given that we are all sinners in need of grace, there must be a better way for us to navigate these rough waters without abandoning God's highest ideal for human sexual expression. To this end, David Bennett wrote about how he concluded his remarks at the interfaith discussion that night:

> "If I could leave everyone in this room with one message, it's that human marriage between one man and one woman is just a reflection of a more fundamental marriage. That's the one between Jesus and his church. There is no sexual or gender minority group, no religious group, that's not invited to his wedding."[24]

At the end of all this arguing and judging, there will be a wedding between Jesus the Bridegroom and his bride, the church. According to Jesus and David Bennett, that's the only marriage that's really going to matter in the end.

In the meantime, Christians are called to strive for holiness in our hearts and our lives, including our sex lives, not because God enjoys depriving us of something we might enjoy, but because, one day, he will give us something far better than any of us can possibly imagine.

Leviticus: The Most Progressive Book in the Bible

I think we all owe Leviticus a huge apology for treating it like an out-of-date disgrace all these years. Does it get weird sometimes? Yeah. A little gross? Maybe. But should we treat Leviticus like it's the standard-bearer for primeval bigotry and xenophobia? Absolutely not. In fact, any honest reading of the Old Testament's third book would show that most people have no idea how radically forward-thinking and inclusive Leviticus really is.

Of all the revolutionary ideas in Scripture, the most radical comes from the twenty-fifth chapter of Leviticus. After God handed down all the rules for his people to live by, he delivered his most extreme mandate. After escaping slavery in Egypt, the Hebrews established a way of life that was built around the God-ordained Sabbath in which the people worked six days a week before resting on the seventh. The same rhythm of six-on, one-off held true annually as well; the Hebrews worked the land for six years, but the seventh year was set aside for rest—for the people, as well as the land (Leviticus 25:1-7).

This is where things get a little crazy. After the seventh, seventh year (or the forty-ninth year), year fifty was intended to be set aside as a super-Sabbath. God commanded that every fiftieth year be a universal reset for his people; among other things, all Hebrews were called to

- return all property accumulated over the past fifty years to its original owner;
- go back to live on their family's ancestral land;

- give the land an extra year of rest, eating only what grows in the wild;
- stop working for a year;
- forgive all debts owed to you;
- release all your slaves;
- release all prisoners of war;
- show extra kindness to poor people, foreigners, strangers, and servants.

This fiftieth year was called the year of *Jubilee*, which literally means "horn of the ram," because at the beginning of that year, the high priest was supposed to blow a ram's horn to start the revolution. *Jubilee* was meant to be the centerpiece of the Hebrew community; it was supposed to set God's people apart from other nations.

Can you imagine a society that actually lived in a Jubilee rhythm? It may seem unrealistic or unsustainable, but I'm not sure that we who live in a nation that's in debt to the tune of twenty-seven trillion dollars (that's $27,000,000,000,000!) and growing should be the experts on sustainability. Maybe the fifty-year reset would change how we live in some good ways. Maybe we'd borrow and lend money differently. Maybe we'd exploit each other less. Maybe we'd see less generational poverty.

We may never know, because the Israelites never once followed through on Jubilee. In the Law of Moses, God handed down over six hundred rules, and his people tried to follow all of them, except Jubilee.

No bacon? *Check!*

No polyester? *Check!*

No sleeping with any of your aunts? *Check!*

The Jubilee year? *crickets*...

Scholars disagree about the reasons why, but the best hypothesis may simply be that, by the time the first, fiftieth year rolled around, Israel's leadership found Jubilee to be too difficult or inconvenient to enforce.[25] But in the absence of Hebrew follow-through, God didn't give up on his vision. Jubilee reappears throughout the rest of the Bible under a different banner: "the year of the Lord's favor." More than seven centuries after God handed down the Law to Moses, God reasserted his vision for Jubilee through the prophet Isaiah:

> *The spirit of the Lord GOD is upon me,*
>> *because the LORD has anointed me;*
> *he has sent me to bring good news to the oppressed,*
>> *to bind up the brokenhearted,*
> *to proclaim liberty to the captives,*
>> *and release to the prisoners;*
>> *to proclaim the year of the LORD's favor. (Isaiah 61:1-2 NRSV)*

And another seven centuries later, Jesus picked up where Isaiah left off. Around age thirty, Jesus left construction work behind and focused all his energy on the gospel movement. One of his first acts as a full-time rabbi took place in his hometown synagogue. While he was there, someone handed him the Isaiah scroll and asked him to read from it. As a rabbi, he was allowed to choose any passage that he wanted. Then:

> *He unrolled the scroll and found the place where it was written:*
>
> *"The Spirit of the Lord is upon me,*

> because he has anointed me
>> to bring good news to the poor.
> He has sent me to proclaim release to the captives
>> and recovery of sight to the blind,
>> to let the oppressed go free,
> to proclaim the year of the LORD's favor."
>
> And he rolled up the scroll, gave it back to the attendant,
> and sat down. The eyes of all in the synagogue were fixed
> on him. Then he began to say to them, "Today this scripture
> has been fulfilled." (Luke 4:17-21 NRSV)

Nearly one thousand, five hundred years after *the year of the Lord's favor* was codified as part of God's Law, Jesus had the audacity to claim that his life represented the arrival of Jubilee. He clearly implied that his life and legacy would bring an end of inequality, slavery, and debt, but has that been the case? Obviously not. Two thousand years later, the world is still as unfair a place as ever. It really begs the question: *Did Jesus fail in his mission to bring Jubilee?*

I don't think so. Seven Sabbaths after his death and resurrection, on the fiftieth day, a Jubilee movement was born. In the book called *Acts of the Apostles*, the Spirit of God moved among a few dozen followers of Jesus and "set them on fire." Two things happened in that moment that defined the Christian movement. First, people who spoke different languages began to understand each other,

What is it about the church that so much of the world has found irresistible for so many years?

and second, all the believers began to share everything they had in common, so that no one went without (Acts 2).

In less than a year, the church grew from a few dozen to several thousand people. Within a few centuries, there were over thirty million Christians on three continents, and today that number has grown to 2.3 billion people of every color and speaking every language in every corner of the world.[26] What is it about the church that so much of the world has found irresistible for so many years?

I think it's Jubilee. In the second century, a Christian leader named Tertullian wrote about how Roman leaders observed the church in action and shook their heads, saying "Look at how they love one another."[27] In the fifth century, the Roman Emperor Julian lamented the fact that Christianity, which he frequently called *atheism* (Julian also frequently referred to Christians as "Jews"), was growing faster than Greco-Roman paganism was. In a letter to a pagan high priest named Arsacius, Julian wrote,

> It is disgraceful that, when no Jew ever has to beg, and the impious Galilaeans support not only their own poor but ours as well, all men see that our people lack aid from us.... Then let us not, by allowing others to outdo us in good works...utterly abandon the reverence due to the gods.[28]

Over the years, Christians have missed the point of church and leaders have abused their power in various, insidious ways. We haven't always gotten it right, but when the church is on target, there is nothing like it in all the world. I believe the church's purpose is connected to the radical society God prescribed in Leviticus 25.

Church is the one place left in the world where no one gets what they pay for. Go to a football game or to the opera, and you'll sit where you can afford to sit. Everyone knows there are some major differences between box seats and standing room only. Church is different. It doesn't matter how much you're worth, or how much you give, or if you have nothing to give, no one gets box seats in the church.

If you give my church a million bucks, and the Smith family gives a hundred, your kids and the Smith kids will still be in the same class on Sunday. You and Mr. Smith will stand in the same line for the same coffee, and you'll each grab donuts from the same box. The same goes for Ms. Jones who needed rental assistance last month, so the church wrote a check to cover her…with part of your million bucks. You and Ms. Jones are still worth exactly the same at church. When the time comes for Holy Communion, you won't get a bigger piece of the body of Christ just because you had more to give. You won't get wine while everyone else drinks Welch's.

In the church, we make sure everyone has enough, and no one goes without. You might be thinking, "That's socialism! Why aren't more Christians socialists?" Here's the thing: Christians don't live this way because we *have* to. We share because we *want* to. That's the way it's always been. Ever since the day that God's Spirit set the first Christian hearts on fire, the church has given itself away for the sake of others by building and running schools, hospitals, and orphanages the world over, educating boys *and* girls, befriending the lonely, defending the fatherless, and empowering the powerless.

Jesus came to be the fulfillment of the Law. The church at its best is Jubilee in action. And that, I think, is what Leviticus is really all about.

CHAPTER EIGHT

WHY IS THE BIBLE
SO BACKWARD?

"I'd probably read the Bible more often," Michael explained by email, "if it had anything to say on the issues I really care about (women's rights, equality, economic justice, etc.) but every time I look at it, all I see are rules and the occasional kitschy story reminding me to be nice."

Michael is twenty-seven years old, highly educated, and deeply skeptical. He attends my church two or three times a month and sends me emails full of argumentative questions and sincere doubts maybe once a quarter, which tells me that, at a minimum, he's open to a conversation about the Bible and Christianity. He's even gotten involved in a small group with other young adults, and everybody in the group loves him because he's genuine and has a generous spirit. My church is full of people like Michael, and I've spoken with several other pastors whose churches are seeing a lot of Michaels too: young adults who are curious, caring, and engaged in various ministries, but still aren't comfortable embracing the Bible or "coming out" as Christians.

So what prevents someone like Michael from becoming a committed Christian? It's all about the issues. A century ago, people in the Western world typically defined their worldviews through some combination of their religious persuasion, economic class, cultural heritage, and national identity. If you were a middle-class American Methodist of European descent in the early twentieth century, for example, your worldview was largely predictable.

But all of that has changed at lightspeed. Denominational membership means nothing anymore and one-third of young Americans (ages 18–29) are proud to be citizens of this country, down from sixty percent of young Americans in 2003.[1] The internet and social media have served to break down some of the barriers that once isolated different cultures and classes of people from one another. In the absence of religious, economic, and cultural foundations, people like Michael are building their entire worldviews on a handful of favored causes such as climate change, the wealth gap, abortion rights, gay rights, trans rights, anti-racism, and socialized healthcare, to name a few examples.

The reason this conversation belongs in a book about the Bible is that people like Michael have determined that the *Good Book* has nothing good to say on these critical issues. In fact, where the Bible does explicitly engage these issues, most secular skeptics have deemed its contributions archaic, if not harmful. Some of the questions I often pose to Michael and others of a similar mindset are:

Have you ever really studied the Bible?

- Have you ever really studied the Bible?
- Have you taken the time to analyze what the scriptures actually say?
- Have you honestly examined these writings in their historical and literary context? Or have you merely adopted the popular, presumptuous, and pervasive anti-Bible narrative in our culture without doing your intellectual due diligence?

Most honest skeptics will answer those questions in order: "No, no, no, and **long pause** maybe yes." In this chapter, we'll take a closer look at the Bible's treatment of the defining issues of our time. Is the Bible really backward to the point of irrelevance, or is there some deep, eternal wisdom in the Scriptures that speaks to the issues people today care about the most?

In the previous chapter, I began addressing some of the contemporary issues about which many modern Americans have very strong opinions. And when our opinions on issues that are sacred to us come into conflict with the Bible, we have to decide what we're going to do about it. Generally, the options before us include:

1. Walk away from the Bible.
2. Change the Bible to make it say what I want it to say.
3. Accept the Bible as God's Truth and seek to change myself.

The third option is obviously what I wish everyone would choose, but let me tell you: it's much easier said than done. After writing about homosexuality in the previous chapter, I felt like I needed a vacation. Sometimes it really hurts to concede "my truth" in favor of God's eternal Truth. In this chapter, I will tackle a few more of the issues that are extremely important to most secular people today.

A Woman's Place

I dealt with the question of misogyny in the Bible in prior chapters, but I doubt that I've said enough about the role of women in Scripture to satisfy the disquieted hearts of my feminist readers. For several decades, outspoken Christian and non-Christian feminists have insisted that the Bible must not be considered a reliable source of objective Truth if only for the fact that it holds women in lower esteem than men.[2]

Given my own history with cynicism, it shouldn't surprise me when I'm talking to a cynic about Christianity and he pulls out the big guns on me: "The Bible is sexist! Look at these verses! Ah-ha! Bet you didn't know these very troubling verses were in this book you've been studying your whole life!"

FYI, cynics—*we know it's in there*. Most of us have known all along, and we leave it there and read it in context because it reminds us that the Bible doesn't shy away from reality. The world is broken, ugly, and mean, and vulnerable people are brutalized every day. The Bible tells that part of the story because, without it, we might forget why this world so badly needs a savior. Though it contains passages that could certainly be considered sexist by today's standards, the Bible is anything but misogynistic.

For years there's been a conflict within Christianity about the role of women in the church. And like most political fights, there are two sides dominating the debate: complementarians believe God assigns certain roles for men, and other roles for women, and any blurring or crossing of those lines is missing the mark of God's ideal for creation. A man's role is to lead, and a woman is to follow his lead and submit to his authority. Egalitarians, on the other hand, believe that, in Christ, there really should be no traditional gender roles, and we should stop boxing men and women into classical definitions of masculinity and femininity.

In complementarian churches, only men are appointed to serve as leaders and elders, while women aren't permitted to lead or teach men because of Bible verses like the one where Paul says, "I do not permit a woman to teach or to assume authority over a man; she must be quiet" (1 Timothy 2:12). But here's the thing: I've been around complementarian churches my whole life, and one thing never fails: behind the scenes of these churches, women are always running things. They run the choir, Sunday school, VBS, weddings, funerals, hospitality, everything. They even run the board meetings by simply sending their husbands as proxies to do their bidding.

"Kenneth, honey, you *will* vote to remove Pastor Karen. Are we clear?"

Egalitarian churches look at other verses, like the one where Paul wrote, "There is no longer male and female; for all of you are one in Christ Jesus" (Galatians 3:28 NRSV), and take it to mean that Jesus canceled out gender roles for Christians. That sounds great in theory, but I've been around these churches too. What tends to happen is that masculinity becomes synonymous with toxic masculinity, and men who are masculine in the traditional sense feel bored at best and unwelcome at worst. All the men who like to do strategic planning and fix up the church building and run the scout troop and play sports with the youth group stop coming, as do many of the women who love them, because many of them are feminine in the classical sense, and they feel judged for dressing a certain way and wearing makeup and serving their husbands.

Biblically speaking, neither egalitarians nor complementarians get it completely right. Complementarians have no answer for all the times in Scripture when God called women like Deborah to lead men and speak on his behalf. In the New Testament, the apostle Paul trusted women to carry his letters and to preach in some of his churches. That's right, the same Paul who ordered women in one congregation to remain silent assumed that women in another congregation were preaching to the church. He wrote, "Every woman who prays or prophesies with her head uncovered dishonors her head" (1 Corinthians 11:5).

The head covering issue can be confusing, but the most important point here is that Paul expected some women to prophesy in some church services. But what did he mean by *prophesy*? Lucky for us, he defined it later in the same letter: "But the one who prophesies speaks to people for their strengthening, encouraging and comfort.... The one who prophesies edifies the church" (1 Corinthians 14:3-4).

That sounds an awful lot like preaching. So which is it—are women supposed to keep silent in church like Paul said to Timothy, or are they supposed to preach with their heads covered like Paul said to the Corinthians? The rules aren't clear, and I believe that whenever the Bible isn't crystal clear about an important issue like this, it's generally a good idea to look to Jesus.

Complementarians and egalitarians will never agree; they're both locked into their dogmas and will be fighting it out on Twitter until the second coming of Christ. That's fine. As for the rest of us who don't fit neatly on either side of that debate, let's look to Jesus to observe how he behaved in the presence of women, how he treated them, and what he expected of them. In the words of Christian scholar Dorothy Sayers:

> Perhaps it is no wonder that the women were first at the Cradle and last at the Cross. They had never known a man like this Man....A prophet and teacher who never nagged at them, never flattered or coaxed or patronised; who never made...jokes about them, never treated them either as "The women, God help us!" or "The ladies, God bless them!"; who rebuked without querulousness and praised without condescension; who took their questions and arguments seriously; who never mapped out their sphere for them, never urged them to be feminine or jeered at them for being female; who had no axe to grind and no uneasy male dignity to defend; who took them as he found them and was completely unself-conscious.[3]

There's something beautiful and good about masculinity, and something beautiful and good about femininity. Men and women uniquely embody the image of God in which we all were created.

Violence in the Bible

After issues relating to sexuality and gender, the questions I hear most often about the Bible pertain to the character of God. Is the God of the Bible really good? In his book, *Letter to a Christian Nation*, atheist author Sam Harris wrote this in response to the kind of catastrophic, violent events that occur all the time on earth, apparently unimpeded by God:

> If God exists, either He can do nothing to stop the most egregious calamities, or He does not care to. God, therefore, is either impotent or evil.[4]

The issue takes on even more urgency when you consider the violence perpetrated in God's name throughout the Bible. The most controversial violence in the Bible is Joshua's military conquest in Jericho and the string of victories that followed:

> *That day Joshua took Makkedah. He put the city and its king to the sword and totally destroyed everyone in it. He left no survivors. And he did to the king of Makkedah as he had done to the king of Jericho.*
>
> *Then Joshua and all Israel with him moved on from Makkedah to Libnah and attacked it. The LORD also gave that city and its king into Israel's hand. The city and everyone in it Joshua put to the sword. He left no survivors there. And he did to its king as he had done to the king of Jericho. (Joshua 10:28-30)*

A passage like this can be even more disturbing when you consider that Joshua was merely following orders. Whose orders? God's. Here's proof:

> However, in <u>the cities of the nations the LORD your God is</u> <u>giving you as an inheritance, do not leave alive anything</u> <u>that breathes. Completely destroy them.</u>... Otherwise, they will teach you to follow all the detestable things they do in worshiping their gods, and you will sin against the LORD your God. (Deuteronomy 20:16-18)

Christians read these kinds of things in the Bible and typically do one of two things. We either say, "Well, God said it. I believe it. Deal with it," which is a brand of biblical interpretation that turns far too many good-hearted, rational people away from the faith. Or we just ignore these parts of scripture, and I'm not sure that's any better. Most people want all the wisdom and love of Jesus without all the violence and blood most often found in the Old Testament. Why can't we have it both ways?

When There Is No Justice

Whenever I hear people expressing this sentiment, I can't help thinking about the summer I spent in Ecuador, visiting my in-laws for the first time. It was the year 2000, and Ecuador's economy was in a tailspin. The government and most businesses were completely shut down. After giving me the grand tour of Quito, my father in-law drove us back to his house, and when we got there, it was clear that his home had been robbed.

While my father in-law was assessing the damage, I went into full *American Hero* mode, barking out orders like, "Somebody call the cops," "Nobody touch anything—*fingerprints, people*," "You'll need a copy of the police report for the insurance claim!" Nobody was listening, so finally I pulled my wife aside and said, "What's going on? Why haven't you called the cops?" Half angry, half sad, she shot back, "Because they're the ones who did it."

The next-door neighbor had seen the whole thing: a few hours before we got home, a bunch of guys rolled up in a police van, kicked the door in, and helped themselves to everything inside.

I started to tell my father-in-law it was time to pay a visit to Internal Affairs at the local precinct, but by then, even I knew that would be naive. In some parts of the world, you can't call the cops. Victims in some communities have no remedy, no recourse, and no hope for justice. All there is to do is pray and keep going.

That's real life for *most* of humanity in the world today, but it was much, much worse for most of humanity three thousand years ago in Joshua's time. It was a savage, barbaric world, far worse than most of us can imagine. The region the Israelites wandered into—Canaan— had been ruled for a few hundred years by the Egyptians, who had devastated the local economies by allowing farmers to grow only a specific kind of grape that the Egyptian elites enjoyed and that could only be grown in Canaan.

Pharaoh ruled with zero tolerance. We have paintings of Pharaoh holding men by their hair with an axe in his hand, preparing to behead them. Because the local economies were shut down, the young men of various tribes formed gangs that wandered the countryside looking for men to rob and women to rape. The gangs were notorious for their guerrilla warfare tactics. We have inscriptions preserved on walls where gang leaders bragged about boring through the bodies of their enemies, creating rivers of blood, flaying the skin off of living victims in full view of their families, cutting the genitalia off of prisoners of war and feeding it to them.

Sometimes the Israelites themselves were the victims of this tribal savagery, like when the Babylonians invaded and destroyed Jerusalem. They burned every home in the city. They captured the Jewish King Zedekiah and his sons. The Babylonian leaders made the king watch as they beheaded his sons, and then they gouged out his eyes to make sure his sons' executions were the last things he ever saw.

So whenever we sit in our twenty-first-century air-conditioned rooms, with our bellies full of food and clean water, and with our children mostly safe and healthy, and we complain about all the nasty violence in the Old Testament, I hear naïveté and privilege. In my experience, almost no one who has a real problem with violence in the Bible has been victimized like people in Bible times were. The ones who criticize God for taking out bad guys in the Old Testament tend to be the same people who can call 9-1-1 when somebody breaks in, people who can trust that justice will be served.

What If Backward Is Actually Forward?

To read the Bible properly is to humbly seek God's heart on every page. As countercultural as this might sound, whenever my feelings on an issue are at odds with something the Bible says, I pray that my heart and mind would stay open to the Spirit of God, that he might give me wisdom to construct my priorities on the foundation of God's Word, rather than building my version of the Bible on the foundation of my priorities.

When approaching the Bible, we must be willing to ask the most uncomfortable questions. Questions like, "What if the Bible isn't backward on the issues? What if I am?"

In so many ways, the Bible truly is backward when compared to "normal" secular culture. The world around us mostly says that wealthy, famous, and powerful people matter more than everyday peasants do, but the Bible says, "God does not show favoritism" (Romans 2:11). From birth, we've been told that nothing matters more than our happiness, but the Bible says holiness is more important than happiness (Matthew 5:48). According to our culture, suffering is bad, but according to Scripture, suffering can be a cause for celebration (Romans 5:3-5). Pleasure and comfort are the aims of this world, but self-denial and sacrifice are among the Bible's highest ideals (John 15:13).

For as long as Christians have walked the earth, the world has called us backward. In the years after the church was born, many Roman officials despised the Christians. The Emperor Nero said it was Christians who set fire to Rome. Roman polemicists accused Christians of everything from atheism to incest to cannibalism—atheism because the Christians refused to bow to Roman idols, incest because the New Testament says "brothers and sisters" should "greet one another with a holy kiss," and cannibalism because of what we say when we serve Communion: "This is the body of Christ; take and eat" (from Matthew 26:26).

Through the years, non-Christians were very critical of the Eucharist because to them it seemed like a bunch of *hocus pocus*. In fact, that's where the phrase *hocus pocus* comes from. In Latin, the phrase "This is my body" is "Hoc est enim corpus meum." The story goes that secular elites used to make fun of Christians by mocking the priests, and over time, they reduced "Hoc est enim corpus meum" to *hocus pocus*.

When you take the time to learn the history behind something like the Last Supper, everything changes. This Christian sacrament is tied to the Seder meal, which Jewish people share every year at Passover as a reminder of how God delivered them from slavery in Egypt. The Seder is intricately choreographed, and every year, for three thousand years, Jewish people have followed the same basic script.

Most Bible readers miss what really happened the night that Jesus served his disciples the Seder in Matthew 26. Every detail of the Seder—every word, every prayer, every bite—has always been the same. Everyone at the table gets four small cups of wine, the first two of which they drink during the meal. After the meal, they take the third cup, which is called the cup of redemption. That's the cup that Jesus took when he said, "Drink from it, all of you. This is my blood of the covenant, which is poured out for many for the forgiveness of sins" (Matthew 26:27-28).

But then, mysteriously, that Seder ended before Jesus and his disciples drank the final cup of wine, known as the cup of completion. Instead, Jesus flipped the script and fled to the Garden of Gethsemane. While he was there, he prayed: "Father,... may this cup be taken from me" (Matthew 26:39), which doesn't make sense

191

unless you understand what just happened at the Seder. The true cup of completion was the cross.

What did the cross of Jesus *complete*? According to the profound New Testament book called Hebrews, the cross completed, or fulfilled, our dependence on religious works as a means of satisfying God's wrath over our sin.

> *Sacrifice for sin is no longer necessary.*
>
> *Therefore, brothers and sisters, since we have confidence to enter the Most Holy Place by the blood of Jesus, ... let us draw near to God with a sincere heart and with the full assurance that faith brings. (Hebrews 10:18-19, 22)*

Before the cross, Jewish people understood the Temple to be the epicenter of their religion, and at the center of the Temple was a room called the Holy of Holies, which Jews believed was the physical home of God. A massive curtain, or veil, provided a symbolic separation between the Holy of Holies and the ordinary people of God. Only certain priests were allowed to enter God's presence inside the Holy of Holies.

Because of Jesus, anyone and everyone is able to approach the presence of God without fear.

But the moment that Jesus breathed his final breath on the cross, Matthew says "the curtain of the temple was torn in two" (Matthew 27:51). The cross was the death knell for humanity's dependence on religious middle-men and compensatory works. Because of

Jesus, anyone and everyone is able to approach the presence of God without fear.

The cross was a revolution.

But Why a Cross?

It's also bizarre, isn't it? Have you ever wondered why Jesus had to take the cross in the first place, and why Christians celebrate the cross every bit as much as we venerate the empty tomb? Volumes have been written about the meaning of the cross and how Jesus's blood atoned for all our sins, and from a biblical standpoint, that is absolutely true. But I also believe that Jesus died on the cross because in the first-century Roman Empire, it was the most backward way to die.

Crucifixion may be the most painful, degrading, and torturous method of state-sanctioned terror in human history. Rome crucified only the worst brand of criminals—those who killed or stole from Roman citizens, and those guilty of treason, including men like Jesus who called themselves kings. The Romans perfected the sadistic art of crucifixion, and they crucified hundreds of convicts per day.

In some ways the crucifixion of Jesus was ordinary. Using leather whips laced with bits of glass, bone, and pottery shards, Roman soldiers flogged most of the men and women they crucified, and they often "cast lots"—or rolled the dice—to determine which soldier would keep the victim's clothes as a trophy. Depending on the convict's crime, soldiers enjoyed inventing ways to humiliate them. In the case of this "King of the Jews," they forced the crown of thorns onto his head and laid a "royal robe" across his bloodied back.

Then they stripped Jesus naked, and forced him to carry his cross, which probably weighed a hundred fifty pounds, to the place where he was executed. Contrary to what you may have heard, Jesus wasn't crucified "on a hill far away," but just outside Jerusalem's gates, near a busy street. Why? Because the Romans didn't just want to kill guys like Jesus; they wanted to humiliate them as much as possible. Matthew's Gospel says that, as Jesus was dying, naked and condemned, people were passing by and insulting him (Matthew 27:39).

The Romans didn't always use nails; sometimes they just tied people to their crosses until they suffocated. But in Jesus's case, they used three or four large nails to attach his body to the wood. The pain of the nails grinding against his bones was undoubtedly excruciating.

Before he died, Jesus told those standing nearby that he was thirsty, and then:

> At once one of them ran and got a sponge, filled it with sour
> wine, put it on a stick, and gave it to him to drink.... Then
> Jesus cried again with a loud voice and breathed his last.
> (Matthew 27:48, 50 NRSV)

Has that ever seemed weird to you? Where did they find a sponge on a stick at a public execution? And why did they give him sour wine instead of water? Archaeologists have long understood that, whenever the Romans conquered a city, they liked to make certain buildings, such as theaters, into public latrines for Roman citizens and soldiers to use.[5]

Archaeologists have also found placards on the walls in some of these Roman latrines with inscriptions that read something like: "Rinse sponge when finished." Here's what we know: Romans used communal sponges in these restrooms, these sponges were on sticks, they were used to wipe their dirty bottoms,[6] and in between uses they were to be rinsed in some kind of disinfectant. What were the most common disinfectants in the first-century Roman Empire? Vinegar, salt water,[7] or, in a pinch, wine.

It's also very likely that Roman soldiers carried a sponge on a stick and some disinfectant with them as part of their supplies, which might explain how somebody came up with a sponge on a stick and some sour wine at a public execution.[8]

Most people think they gave Jesus a drink as an act of mercy, but perhaps it wasn't mercy at all. Perhaps it was the most disgusting, degrading kind of insult. If, in fact, they made Jesus drink from their toilet sponge, that was the last thing he did before he died.

Stories don't get more backward than this, so it would seem it's a story that Christians would be eager to forget. But in the years following Jesus's death, Christian leaders like Paul constantly championed the cross. "We preach Christ crucified," Paul wrote, "a stumbling block to Jews and foolishness to Gentiles" (1 Corinthians 1:23).

To religious men like Paul, part of what made the cross such a scandal was the Bible itself. Deuteronomy 21:23 (NRSV) says that "Anyone hung on a tree is under God's curse." So if the Bible is true, then Jesus was cursed. That is the reason why Paul preached "Christ crucified," which literally means "Cursed Savior" or "Damned Messiah."

What kind of God allows himself to be cursed? What kind of God could ever be damned?

Only Jesus, the God who is love. This God may seem backward to us, but I've learned that it's usually me who is backward. Whenever

I'm facing the wrong direction, everything that's right will seem wrong to me.

Although Jesus was totally righteous, he chose to carry my unrighteousness. Although he was innocent, he gladly took the cross so the whole world can know that he took our sin and shame to the grave with him. And now, every curse is broken. Every fear is gone. And because he rose in glory, so will we.

CONCLUSION

I've suggested several times throughout this book that what we do with the Bible depends entirely upon what we choose to believe about Jesus of Nazareth. Obviously he was a great teacher who made an immeasurable impact on the world, but that doesn't make him unique. That fact alone would mean Jesus belongs in a category of gurus alongside Muhammed, the Dalai Lama, and other great spiritual leaders in history.

Some skeptics have surmised that Jesus was a great teacher whose disciples, in the aftermath of the cross, refused to let him die. In their grief, perhaps they mythologized their leader, posthumously promoting him from gifted teacher to sovereign Lord.

But given everything we've covered in this book, what do you believe to be true about Jesus?

Was he just a man whose followers made him a legend?

Or was he something more?

Jesus: Man, Myth, or *Monomyth*?

In the mid-twentieth century, a brilliant scholar named Joseph Campbell spent decades studying and scrutinizing the stories people tell, paying special attention to the thousands of epic stories that have appeared in every religion and culture since the dawn of time. Chinese, Sumerians, Egyptians, Babylonians, Israelites, Greeks, Romans—every civilization has repeated stories about their heroes. After studying these myths for decades, Joseph Campbell realized that all of the myths told among the world's various cultures are essentially the same story, and the protagonists are all essentially the same hero.

In 1949, Campbell wrote a book called *The Hero with a Thousand Faces*, in which he mapped out the path that every mythical hero takes in every cultural mythology.[1] It's a journey that will likely sound familiar, especially if you love epic books and movies. The first step in the hero's journey is the "Call to Adventure," in which we're introduced to the hero before he or she becomes a hero (think about Luke Skywalker enjoying a normal childhood on Tatooine).

Sooner or later, the hero is helped along by an eccentric friend who has some special knowledge, and this friend encourages the hero to be who he or she really is (imagine Hagrid coming to rescue Harry Potter from the Dursleys). There comes a moment, though, when our hero has to choose to be a hero (picture Neo faced with the choice to take the red pill) and knows that once this decision is made, there can be no going back (recall Katniss Everdeen screaming "I volunteer as tribute!" to save her sister's life).

Once our hero accepts the mission, he or she is led by a spiritual guide to a remote place and endures some kind of training, including a test (like the time Yoda trained Luke on Planet Dagobah). After passing the test, our hero realizes just how dangerous the journey will be and knows he or she must face the hero's worst fear (picture Frodo staring at fiery Mount Doom from a distance).

Even though afraid, our hero marches on, until all hell breaks loose, and the enemy appears to have won (Enter Thanos, snapping his fingers). In a last-ditch effort to save the world, the hero goes straight into the belly of the beast, but the darkness is too strong to overcome, so the hero lays down his or her life for the hero's friends (such as when Harry went alone to face Voldemort, knowing that he'd be killed).

But not even death can keep our hero down, for just when all hope seems lost, he or she rises up and deals the final blow to the Villain who sought to hold the hero's people captive (picture Rey using Luke and Leia's lightsabers to kill Emperor Palpatine once and for all). Once the mission is complete, our hero leaves the world he or she came to save (remember when Frodo left the Shire after saving it?) until the appointed time when our hero will return in glory. And one day, in the end, the rightful ruler will be crowned, evil will be vanquished, and there will be peace on earth at last (like when T'Challa was finally crowned King of Wakanda).

Harry Potter, The Matrix, Black Panther, The Avengers, Star Wars, The Hunger Games—these are all myths and legends. Joseph Campbell believed that all human myths are derivative variants of the same, true story, which he called the *Monomyth*. How else could so many different cultures speaking different languages at different times and places all tell such similar versions of the same story?

So, what about Jesus? His story sounds a lot like Campbell's mythical hero. Is his saga derivative of other source material, or is he the Source? Is he merely a myth, or is Jesus the *Monomyth*?

- His story might follow the same pattern myths do, but with some very important distinctions. First, he was a historical figure and not a fictional character. Second, the stories we have about Jesus were written within decades of his life—not hundreds of years later—by people who knew him, not distant philosophers.

- Mythologies magnify the pre-existing worldview of their culture; Jesus's story presented an existential threat to the first-century Jewish worldview. The Hebrew Scriptures were clear: God was in the heavens, and no man could ever be God. So it's safe to assume that, if Jewish people were going to create a mythology to bolster their religion, they would never have come up with a man from Nazareth who was God in the flesh.

You can trust him. And if you can trust Jesus, you can also trust the Bible that attests to him.

These are all very good reasons to believe that Jesus isn't merely another myth. He is the *Monomyth*, the Messiah. He's not derivative of some other source material; he is the Source. You can trust him. And if you can trust Jesus, you can also trust the Bible that attests to him.

I loved the Bible as a child. I left it in my teens. I hated it in my 20s. I came back to it in my 30s, and now I'm more aware than ever of how lost I'd be without this book. It's not just the *Good Book*. It's the perfect story about the perfect God's perfect love for imperfect people like you and me.

> *The Bible is not an end in itself, but a means to bring us to an intimate and satisfying knowledge of God.*
>
> —A.W. Tozer[2]

RESOURCES
FOR PERSONAL REFLECTION
AND GROUP DISCUSSION

Chapter One: Isn't the Bible Only Human?

- Have you ever experienced the combativeness of insecure Christians who disagreed with you? What effect did that experience have on you?
- How does my explanation of the Cain's wife conundrum (Genesis 1-4 are not eyewitness reports, it's not important whom Cain married, all that matters is God's love for Cain) sit with you? How do you think Christians should respond when faced with a question like, "Whom did Cain marry?"
- Do the moral deficiencies of the Bible characters add to your trust in Scripture, or take away from it? Why?
- How did Jesus come to correct what Cain got wrong?
- How is the gospel of Jesus distinct from the negative problem-solving that is so commonly found in religions?

Bible Study Tip 1: Context

Read Psalm 51:1-17. King David wrote this psalm after committing a series of truly awful sins (2 Samuel 11). First, he commanded a woman who was not his wife to have sex with him. Then, after learning that she was pregnant, he arranged for her husband to be killed. After that, David pretended to be a benevolent hero by taking the poor widow into his own home.

How does knowing the backstory help you to better understand Psalm 51?

Chapter Two: Is the Bible Fact or Fiction?

- Does the fact that flawed human beings wrote the Bible diminish your respect or appreciation for Scripture? Why or why not?
- How does learning about the "oral tradition" affect your confidence in the Bible? Why?
- How does understanding the Bible as one big story help you make sense of hard-to-read passages?
- How much does it matter to you that the Bible is so well-substantiated compared to other ancient texts? Explain.

Bible Study Tip 2: Genre

Whether you're reading a book, a website, or Twitter, it's always important to keep in mind the genre of the text in front of you. We have been trained to read serious news reports, steamy romantic novels, emails from friends, and history books through very different lenses.

The Bible is comprised of at least nine different literary genres: History, Law, Poetry, Narrative, Wisdom, Prophecy, Biography, Correspondence, and Apocalyptic Literature. Learning to read the Bible means discerning which genre you're reading at any given time, so you can apply the correct interpretive lens to the text in question. Here are a few tips to keep in mind:

- Whenever entire blocks of text are indented, such as in the Psalms, you're reading poetry or songs meant for worship and prayer.

- Everything in the New Testament from Romans through Jude is correspondence; you're literally reading someone else's mail. It's helpful to remember that you're seeing only one side of a two-way conversation.

- Proverbs and Ecclesiastes are good examples of Wisdom Literature: collections of wise sayings that are meant to shape their readers' moral and ethical lives.

- Genesis 1–11—the stories of Creation, the Flood, and the Tower of Babel—are probably best understood as Narrative Literature: stories that are likely based on historical events but are primarily intended to teach theology, not history.

- The books of Isaiah, Jeremiah, Ezekiel, and the twelve "Minor Prophets" (Hosea through Malachi) are Prophetic Literature, which means they offer scathing pronouncements of God's judgment, as well as comforting words of grace, as they share visions from God about Israel's future.

Chapter Three: Are the Gospels Reliable?

- What's the difference between *facts* and *truth*, and why does that distinction matter when thinking about the Bible?

- Do you agree with the premise that the legitimacy of Christianity rests on the actual, physical resurrection of Jesus from the dead? Why or why not?

- Where do you find yourself in Peter's story?

- Which of the four Gospels resonates with you the most and why?

- If the Gospel of John was written so much later than the other three, why do you think it should be valued as highly as Matthew, Mark, and Luke?

Bible Study Tip 3: Know Your Gospels

In this chapter, we explored the particular angles and agendas of each of the four Gospel writers. Can you sum up the distinct approaches that Matthew, Mark (Peter), Luke, and John took when telling the story of Jesus's life, death, and resurrection? What was their particular purpose in writing a Gospel?

- Mark (Peter)
- Matthew
- Luke
- John

Chapter Four: What Is the Bible About?

- Why do you think so few people today believe the Bible is a love story?
- Do you agree with my assessment that love is the one common thematic thread that runs throughout all of Scripture? Why or why not?
- What did you think of how Richard Dawkins explained love to his daughter?
- Why is the phrase "God is love" the most extraordinary claim in all the Bible?
- Have you, like Leah, ever settled for lesser forms of love? How did that work out for you?

Bible Study Tip 4: Expect Love on Every Page

People can find just about anything they're looking for in the Bible. If you open the Bible in search of reasons to close it and walk away, that's what you'll find. If you read the Bible looking for crazy verses that you can quote to make Christians feel stupid, you'll probably find some.

Part of trusting Jesus means opening your Bible and expecting to find real love on every page. When you look for love in Scripture, you'll find it, and it will blow your mind. Once you see God's love in the Bible, you can't unsee it. And then you'll begin to see how immature you were when you made fun of the Bible based on a few strange, cherry-picked passages. Even when you come across something that seems impossible to reconcile with a God who is love, keep searching, asking questions, and praying for God's Spirit to give you eyes to see his love on every page.

Chapter Five: Why Is the Bible So Messy?

- "Many of the stories and laws in the Bible fall painfully short of the moral perfection we might expect from a book that claims to be inspired by the one true God." How did this line sit with you? How have the stories that contain blatant immorality (genocide, sexism, slavery, and so forth) impacted your view of the Bible?

- What does it say about God that he saw a woman like Tamar, that he sided with her in the conflict with Judah, and that he blessed her doubly in the end?

- What do you think about the image of the Bible as impressionist art? Have you ever been discouraged or confused when reading the Bible because you "zoomed in" too close on a few small parts? What happened when you stepped back to see the fuller picture?

- What were some of the running themes throughout the Bible stories covered in this chapter (Tamar and Judah, the Levite and the Concubine, and Jesus and the bleeding woman)?

- How were Virgie's cream-taters symbolic of God's grace in Jesus Christ?

Bible Study Tip 5: Pray the Scriptures

Oftentimes, the same people who struggle to understand the Bible also struggle with prayer. One obvious solution is to learn how to pray the scriptures. Here's how it works:

- Choose a passage to pray. The Psalms are a good place to start, but so are the Proverbs, portions of Paul's letters (for example, Romans 5:2-5, Galatians 3:28, or Romans 12:1-2), or the Sermon on the Mount (Matthew 5-7).
- Read the passage (out loud, preferably).
- Either let that passage be your prayer to God, or offer a simple prayer based on that passage (such as, "Lord, help me to learn from this passage today by _____.")

Chapter Six: Is the Bible Racist?

- Have you ever had an experience like the one I had in Korea—one that opened your eyes and stretched your horizons? What did that experience teach you about God and Truth?
- How can we be sure that diversity was always important to God in the Bible?
- How might *scattering*—being forced to venture outside of our comfort zones—be good for us?
- What does the story of Simeon the eunuch say about the scope of Jesus's mission?
- What can Christians do to combat the sin of racism?

Bible Study Tip 6: Allow Scripture to Change Your Mind

One way that many people hit a proverbial wall when reading scripture is by bringing all our preconceived beliefs, core values, and political views to the Bible, fully expecting the Bible to fit like a glove inside our worldview. This leads to all kinds of existential angst because the ideals presented in scripture leave no one unscathed. No matter whether you're a Republican or a Democrat, conservative or liberal, wealthy or poor, the Bible will challenge and convict you by setting a higher standard. One important step in the believer's journey is learning to allow the Bible to shape our values and politics, instead of trying to reshape what the Bible says *through* our values and politics.

One simple example of this is found in the Sermon on the Mount, where Jesus addressed the adulterers in his audience. He said,

"You have heard that it was said, 'You shall not commit adultery.' But I tell you that whoever looks at a woman lustfully has already committed adultery with her in his heart" (Matthew 5:27-28).

Almost everyone agrees that adultery is bad, and that adulterers should be ashamed. But consider Jesus's message here, and how it reshapes the concept of adultery. How should this change the way we think about sin in general?

Name one or two ways in which the Bible has changed your mind about something.

Chapter Seven:
Can We Talk about Leviticus?

- Name a few things you commonly heard or assumed about Leviticus before reading this chapter. Did this chapter change the way you see Leviticus? How?

- Why is context so important when interpreting a book like Leviticus? What was the context in which Leviticus was written?

- Why do you think so few people take Leviticus seriously?

- The Bible obviously has a reputation for being sex-negative. How would you describe the Bible's general position on human sexuality?

- Do you agree with my premise that, at its best, the church is the closest thing to Jubilee the world has ever known? Why or why not?

Bible Study Tip 7: Read the Bible in Community

The Bible was written by community, in community, and for community. Most of it was written during times when very few people were literate, so it was meant to be read aloud in groups. While there's certainly nothing wrong with reading the Bible alone, the real magic happens when you engage the scriptures with others. If you don't have that kind of community in your life, I encourage you to seek it out. If you have trouble finding a group that works for you, email me (office@erichuffman.org) and we'll connect you to one of our online Bible classes.

Chapter Eight:
Why Is the Bible So Backward?

- What contemporary social issues are most important to you, and why? Do you see the Bible as a friend or foe in relation to these issues?

- How would you respond to the three questions I like to pose to skeptics like Michael?

  » Have you ever really studied the Bible?

  » Have you taken the time to analyze what the scriptures actually say?

  » Have you honestly examined these writings in context, or have you merely adopted the popular, presumptuous, and pervasive anti-Bible narrative in our culture without doing your intellectual due diligence?

- What are some of the "issues" near to your heart that you struggle to reconcile with the Bible? How have those issues kept you from engaging more fully with scripture?

- How were the life and death of Jesus "backward" from this world's perspective? What does that tell you about how our social norms compare with the holiness of God?

Bible Study Tip 8: Memorize a Bible Verse Every Week

When we were kids, adults made us memorize stuff all the time, because they knew memorization skills are an important way that we learn. For some reason, when we grow up, we stop memorizing important things. This has been especially true since the dawn of the iPhone era. Our devices, along with Google, now remember everything for us.

That's why, now more than ever, memorization can be a powerful tool when reading the Bible. I recommend that, every Sunday night, you choose a verse or two of scripture to memorize, and repeat that verse as much as possible throughout the week. The better you get at memorizing Bible passages, the longer or more challenging your memory verses can become. As a bonus, you'll be surprised how many of your memory verses will come in handy when talking about life with the people God puts in your path.

Notes

Prologue

1. Ask your parents, kids!
2. Learn more in Virgilio Corbo, *The House of St. Peter at Capharnaum* (Jerusalem: Franciscan Printing Press, 1969), 54–55, 67–70.

Chapter One: Isn't the Bible Only Human?

1. "Hebrew Bible" is a slightly more respectful way of saying the Old Testament, but I tend to use "Old Testament" for simplicity's sake.
2. Joan E. Taylor, *What Did Jesus Look Like?* (London: Bloomsbury T&T Clark, 2018), 155–159.
3. Alan Hirsch and Mark Nelson, *Reframation: Seeing God, People, and Mission Through Reenchanted Frames* (Los Angeles: 100 Movements Publishing, 2019), ebook Loc 885 of 5373.

Chapter Two: Is the Bible Fact or Fiction?

1. Adam McCann, "Most Diverse Cities in the U.S.," WalletHub, April 10, 2019, https://wallethub.com/edu/most-diverse-cities/12690/#detailed.
2. Gray Johnson Poole, "Sir Flinders Petrie: British Archaeologist," *Encyclopædia Britannica*, updated July 24, 2020, https://www.britannica.com/biography/Flinders-Petrie.
3. Robb Andrew Young, *Hezekiah in History and Tradition* (Leiden, The Netherlands: Brill, 2012), 48–50.
4. Read a detailed account of the discovery in *The Cyrus Cylinder: The King of Persia's Proclamation from Ancient Babylon*, ed. Irving Finkel (London: I. B. Tauris, 2013).
5. "Cyrus Cylinder Translation," Livius.org, posted in 1998, modified July 13, 2020, https://www.livius.org/sources/content/cyrus-cylinder/cyrus-cylinder-translation/.
6. Martin Beckford, "Richard Dawkins Interested in Setting Up 'Atheist Free School,'" *The Telegraph*, June 24, 2010, www.telegraph.co.uk/news/religion/7849563/Richard-Dawkins-interested-in-setting-up-atheist-free-school.html.

7. *The Wolf of Wall Street*, directed by Martin Scorsese (2013; Hollywood, CA: Paramount Pictures), https://www.paramountmovies.com/movies/the-wolf-of-wall-street.

8. Flavius Josephus, "Chapter 2. How Herod And Philip Built Several Cities In Honor Of Cæsar. Concerning The Succession Of Priests And Procurators; As Also What Befell Phraates And The Parthians," Book XVIII, in *The Antiquities of the Jews*, Project Gutenberg, release date January 4, 2009, last update August 9, 2017, https://www.gutenberg.org/files/2848/2848-h/2848-h.htm.

9. Bernhard W. Anderson, *Understanding the Old Testament*, 4th ed. (Upper Saddle River, NJ: Prentice Hall, 1997), 19.

10. Paul's thirteen letters—Romans, 1 and 2 Corinthians, Galatians, Ephesians, Philippians, Colossians, 1 and 2 Thessalonians, 1 and 2 Timothy, Titus, and Philemon—account for almost half of the New Testament books. Peter (a.k.a. "Satan" from Matthew 16:23) wrote two letters—1 and 2 Peter—and some early Christian leaders, as well as some scholars today, believe that he is the source of Mark's Gospel. I discuss this idea further in chapter 3.

11. The *apocryphal* books were written around or soon after 300 BC and were not included in the Old Testament canon. Still, they are included in some Bibles because of their proximity to biblical events. They do not contradict the biblical narrative in any significant way. In addition to Bel and the Dragon, the Judeo-Christian Apocrypha usually includes Tobit, Judith, 1 and 2 Maccabees, and others.

12. Most Bible scholars define "ancient" as pre-AD 350.

13. See F. F. Bruce, "The Last Thirty Years," in Frederic Kenyon, *The Story of the Bible: A Popular Account of How It Came to Us*, 2nd ed. (Grand Rapids, MI: Eerdmans, 1964). The Book of Esther was the only Old Testament book not found among the scrolls in Qumran.

14. James Arlandson, "New Testament Manuscripts: Discovery and Classification," American Thinker, February 24, 2007, http://www.americanthinker.com/2007/02/new_testament_manuscripts_disc.html.

15. See also Paul D. Wegner, *A Student's Guide to Textual Criticism of the Bible: Its History, Methods and Results* (Downers Grove, IL: InterVarsity Press, 2006).

16. Bart D. Ehrman, *Misquoting Jesus: The Story Behind Who Changed the Bible and Why* (New York: HarperSanFrancisco, 2005), 55.

Chapter Three: Are the Gospels Reliable?

1. David Otto interviewed by Eric Huffman, "Can Faith and Doubt Coexist? (Part One)," June 29, 2018, in *Maybe God Podcast*, season 2, produced by Julie Mirlicourtois, podcast, at 30:39, https://maybegodpod.com/can-faith-and-doubt-coexist-part-one/.

2. A. W. Geiger, "5 Facts on How Americans View the Bible and Other Religious Texts," Pew Research Center, April 14, 2017, https://www.pewresearch.org/fact-tank/2017/04/14/5-facts-on-how-americans-view-the-bible-and-other-religious-texts/.

3. "Chapter XXXIX.—The Writings of Papias" in *The Church History of Eusebius*, Book 3 Chapter 39, Christian Classics Ethereal Library, https://www.ccel.org/ccel/schaff/npnf201.iii.viii.xxxix.html. See also Book 2 Chapter 15; Book 6 Chapter 14.

4. Irenaeus of Lyons, *Against Heresies,* Book 3 Chapter 1, Early Christian Writings, http://www.earlychristianwritings.com/text/irenaeus-book3.html.

5. In Matthew 17:27, Jesus gave Simon Peter money to go and pay the Temple Tax. Every male Jew over the age of 20 had to pay this tax, and this passage suggests that only Jesus and Simon were concerned with paying it. More than likely, the other eleven disciples were under 20 years of age.

6. Yeah, I'm paraphrasing.

7. Here, as in other places, Paul referred to Simon by his Greek name, Cephas.

8. A good example of this is the *Parable of the Vineyard Workers*, found in Matthew 20:1-16.

Chapter Four: What Is the Bible About?

1. Jesus quoted or alluded to 23 Old Testament books.

2. Barna Group, "State of the Bible 2019: Trends in Engagement," Barna, April 18, 2019, https://www.barna.com/research/state-of-the-bible-2019/.

3. Richard Dawkins, *The God Delusion* (Boston: Houghton Mifflin Company, 2006), 31.

4. Thomas Paine, "Age of Reason Letters: I. An Answer to a Friend," May 12, 1797, Thomas Paine National Historical Association, http://thomas paine.org/essays/religion/age-of-reason-letters.html.

5. Christopher Hitchens, *God Is Not Great: How Religion Poisons Everything* (New York: Twelve, 2007), 102.

6. Richard Dawkins, *A Devil's Chaplain: Reflections on Hope, Lies, Science, and Love* (Boston: Houghton Mifflin Company, 2003), 241–242.

Chapter Five: Why Is the Bible So Messy?

1. I highly recommend you take a break to go read about this law, and *The Family of the Unsandaled*, in Deuteronomy 25:5-10!

2. Frank White interviewed in Gary Jordan, "The Overview Effect," episode 107, recorded June 11, 2019, in *Houston We Have a Podcast*, ed. Norah Moran, podcast, https://www.nasa.gov/johnson/HWHAP/ the-overview-effect.

3. Edgar Mitchell in *Overview*, directed by Guy Reid (Planetary Collective, 2016), at 6:52, https://vimeo.com/55073825?utm_campaign=5370367 &utm_source=affiliate&utm_channel=affiliate&cjevent=4fadb94a70f 511ea819a00f60a1c0e11.

4. Nicole Stott in *Overview*, at 3:02, https://vimeo.com/55073825?utm _campaign=5370367&utm_source=affiliate&utm_channel=affiliate& cjevent=4fadb94a70f511ea819a00f60a1c0e11.

5. Ron Garan, *The Orbital Perspective: Lessons in Seeing the Big Picture from a Journey of Seventy-One Million Miles* (Oakland, CA: Berrett-Koehler, 2015), 3–4.

6. Many thanks to Dr. Jo Vitale for opening my eyes to the truth behind this story in her sermon, "Is the Bible Sexist?" on December 16, 2019, at The Story Church in Houston.

Chapter Six: Is the Bible Racist?

1 "Eunuchs," Gwern.net, https://www.gwern.net/docs/rotten.com/ library/sex/castration/eunuch/index.html.

2. St. Irenaeus, *Against Heresies*, ed. Paul Böer Sr. (Veritatis Splendor Publications, 2012), 332–333. Square brackets in Böer; curly brackets added.

3. James Baldwin, *The Negro in American Culture* (1961), ThePostArchive, January 17, 2016, at 0:52, https://www.youtube.com/watch?v=jNpitd JSXWY&feature=youtu.be.

4. Rudy Rasmus interviewed in Eric Huffman, "What Lives Matter?," February 10, 2018, *Maybe God Podcast*, season 1, produced by Julie Mirlicourtois, podcast, https://maybegodpod.com/what-lives-matter/.

5. Esau McCaulley interviewed in Eric Huffman, "Is God Colorblind?," August 21, 2020, *Maybe God Podcast*, season 4, produced by Julie Mirlicourtois, podcast, at 41:38, https://maybegodpod.com/ is-god-colorblind/.

6. Esau McCaulley, "What the Bible Has to Say about Black Anger," *The New York Times*, June 14, 2020, https://www.nytimes.com/2020/06/14/ opinion/george-floyd-psalms-bible.html.

7. McCaulley in "Is God Colorblind?," at 38:00, https://maybegodpod .com/is-god-colorblind/.

Chapter Seven: Can We Talk about Leviticus?

1. C. S. Lewis, *An Experiment in Criticism* (New York: Cambridge University Press, 1961), chapter 7, page 73.

2. Except two of my favorite low-key heroes in Scripture, Shiphrah and Puah. Find their story in Exodus 1:15-22.

3. Read about how God freed the Hebrew slaves in Exodus 14.

4. Noah Wiener, "Bronze Age Collapse: Pollen Study Highlights Late Bronze Age Drought," Biblical Archaeology Society, June 28, 2020, https://www.biblicalarchaeology.org/daily/news/bronze-age-collapse -pollen-study-highlights-late-bronze-age-drought/.

5. If eradicating dangerous mold and mildew is of interest to you, read Leviticus 13:47-59 and 14:33-57.

6. Recent studies indicate that about 50 percent of adults are OK with this act.

7. OK, this rule seems out of place but I still think most people today would agree with it.

8. Tom W. Smith, "Public Attitudes Toward Homosexuality," NORC/ University of Chicago, September 2011, https://www.norc.org/PDFs/ 2011%20GSS%20Reports/GSS_Public%20Attitudes%20Toward%20 Homosexuality_Sept2011.pdf (PDF).

9. "The Partisan Divide on Political Values Grows Even Wider: Homosexuality, Gender and Religion," Pew Research Center, October 5, 2017, https://www.pewresearch.org/politics/2017/10/05/5-homosexuality-gender-and-religion/.

10. Katy Steinmetz, "See Obama's 20-Year Evolution on LGBT Rights," TIME, April 10, 2015, https://time.com/3816952/obama-gay-lesbian-transgender-lgbt-rights/.

11. Also commonly called *Song of Solomon*.

12. Dan B. Allender and Tremper Longman III, *Intimate Allies: Rediscovering God's Design for Marriage and Becoming Soul Mates for Life* (Carol Stream, IL: Tyndale House, 1999), 253–254, quoted in Timothy Keller, *The Meaning of Marriage: Facing the Complexities of Commitment with the Wisdom of God* (2011; New York: Penguin Books, 2013), chapter 8. Square brackets in Keller; curly brackets added. For Longman's commentary on Song of Songs 5, see Tremper Longman III, *The New International Commentary on the Old Testament: Song of Songs*, ed. Robert L. Hubbard Jr. (Grand Rapids, MI: Eerdmans: 2001).

13. It is important to note here that Paul is addressing marriages between believers who love Jesus and are thus committed to the gospel and all the love, gentleness, and respect it fosters in us. We do not believe that this "When your spouse wants it, you better give it up" rule applies to marriages where Jesus is not at the center.

14. Philip Yancey, *Rumors of Another World: What on Earth Are We Missing?* (Grand Rapids, MI: Zondervan, 2003), chapter 5.

15. M. Daspe, M. Vaillancourt-Morel, Y. Lussier, S. Sabourin, and A. Ferron (2017), "When Pornography Use Feels Out of Control: The Moderation Effect of Relationship and Sexual Satisfaction," *Journal of Sex & Marital Therapy* 44, no. 4 (2018): 343–353, https://doi.org/10.1080/0092623X.2017.1405301 (restricted access). A *Psychology Today* article reports on this research at https://www.psychologytoday.com/us/blog/experimentations/201802/when-is-porn-use-problem.

16. Jane Randel and Amy Sánchez, "Parenting in the Digital Age of Pornography," *The Huffington Post*, February 26, 2016, updated February 26, 2017, https://www.huffpost.com/entry/parenting-in-the-digital-age-of-pornography_b_9301802.

17. Stephanie Enson, "Evaluating the Impact of Pornography on the Lives of Children and Young People," *British Journal of School Nursing* 12, no. 7 (September 2017): 326–330, posted October 12, 2017, https://doi.org/10.12968/bjsn.2017.12.7.326 (restricted access).

18. Peter Moore, "Young Americans Are Less Wedded to Monogamy Than Their Elders," YouGov.com, October 3, 2016, https://today.yougov.com/topics/lifestyle/articles-reports/2016/10/03/young-americans-less-wedded-monogamy.

19. Moore, "Young Americans Are Less Wedded to Monogamy."

20. *The Parable of the Wedding Banquet* in Luke 14:15-24 is one example of many.

21. Adam Hamilton, *Making Sense of the Bible* (New York: HarperCollins, 2014), 270–271.

22. N. T. Wright interviewed in John Allen Jr., "Interview with Anglican Bishop N. T. Wright of Durham, England," *National Catholic Reporter*, May 21, 2004, posted May 28, 2004, https://www.nationalcatholicreporter.org/word/wright.htm.

23. David Bennett, *A War of Loves: The Unexpected Story of a Gay Activist Discovering Jesus* (Grand Rapids, MI: Zondervan, 2018), 220–221.

24. Bennett, *A War of Loves*, 221–222.

25. William Baur, "Jubilee Year," *International Standard Bible Encyclopedia*, ed. James Orr (Chicago: The Howard-Severance Company, 1915).

26. Rodney Stark, *The Rise of Christianity: How the Obscure, Marginal Jesus Movement Became the Dominant Religious Force in the Western World in a Few Centuries* (Princeton, NJ: Princeton University Press, 1996).

27. Entry of "Tertullian," from *Apologeticus*, ch. 39, sect. 7, in *Oxford Essential Quotations*, 4th ed. (Oxford: Oxford University Press, 2016).

28. Julian, *Letters*, Letter 22, translated by Emily Wilmer Cave Wright, from *The Works of the Emperor Julian*, Vol. III (New York: G. P. Putnam's Sons, 1913). Judea was such a remote and unimportant territory that Roman officials often conflated "Jews" and "Christians" due to their ignorance.

Chapter Eight: Why Is the Bible So Backward?

1. Jeffrey M. Jones, "New Low of 52% 'Extremely Proud' to Be Americans," Gallup, July 1, 2016, https://news.gallup.com/poll/193379/new-low-extremely-proud-americans.aspx.

2. For examples of Christian feminist critiques of Scripture, check out the work of Rosemary Radford Ruether and Letty Russell.

3. Dorothy L. Sayers, *Are Women Human? Penetrating, Sensible, and Witty Essays on the Role of Women in Society* (1971; Grand Rapids, MI: Eerdmans, 2005), 68.

4. Sam Harris, *Letter to a Christian Nation* (2006; New York: First Vintage Books, 2008), 55.

5. Ann Olga Koloski-Ostrow, "Talking Heads: What Toilets and Sewers Tell Us about Ancient Roman Sanitation," The Conversation, November 19, 2015, https://theconversation.com/talking-heads-what-toilets-and -sewers-tell-us-about-ancient-roman-sanitation-50045.

6. Julie Beck, "Roman Plumbing: Overrated," *The Atlantic*, January 8, 2016, https://www.theatlantic.com/health/archive/2016/01/ancient-roman -toilets-gross/423072/?gclid=CjwKCAjw5p_8BRBUEiwAPpJO6yvZF_ ucbTYRw24D9o6b6w4EhJOG2CBssNztDONBG7fg6BWRSKVVGRo C_DsQAvD_BwE.

7. Erin Blakemore, "What Did People Do Before Toilet Paper?," *National Geographic*, March 31, 2020, https://www.nationalgeographic.com/ history/2020/03/what-people-do-before-toilet-paper/#close. This article also recounts the suicide of a Roman gladiator "who shoved a stick tipped with a sponge 'devoted to the vilest uses' down his throat rather than head into the arena to die by wild animal."

8. Bert Gary, "Was Jesus Crucified in the Manner Shown in Paintings and Movies?," *Infinity Now* (blog), January 24, 2009, https://bertgary .blogspot.com/2009/01/was-jesus-crucified-in-manner-shown-in.html.

Conclusion

1. Joseph Campbell, *The Hero with a Thousand Faces*, 3rd ed., The Collected Works of Joseph Campbell series (1949; Novato, CA: New World Library, 2008).

2. A. W. Tozer, *The Pursuit of God* (Harrisburg, PA: Christian Publications Inc., 1948), adapted from the Preface, Project Gutenberg, released April 23, 2008, https://www.gutenberg.org/files/25141/25141-h/25141-h.htm.